Creativ

CW00687954

APPLE

Creative Cloth Doll Making

New Approaches for Using Fibre, Beads, Dyes, and Other Exciting Techniques

Patti Medaris Culea
Designed by Peter King & Company

APPLE

Published in the UK in 2003 by
Apple Press
Sheridan House
112-116A Western Road
Hove
East Sussex BN3 1DD

ISBN 1-84092-403-9
10 9 8 7 6 5 4 3

Design and Layout: Peter King & Company
Cover Design: Peter King & Company
Cover Image: Bobbie Bush Photography,
www.bobbiebush.com
Doll Portraits: Bobbie Bush Photography,
www.bobbiebush.com
Step Photography: Hirsch Design
Step Illustrator: Judy Love
Pattern Illustrator: Roberta Frauwirth
Project Manager/Copy Editor: Stacey Ann Follin
Proofreader: Karen Comerford

Printed in Singapore

Contents

Introduction   8

Chapter 1   The Basics: Exploring key techniques   10

Chapter 2   Surfaces and Coloration: Working with dyes, paints, and stamps   20

Chapter 3   Fabrications: Working with Tyvek, liners, and machine embroidery   40

Chapter 4   Beading: Doing peyote beadwork and bead embroidery   64

Chapter 5   Collage: Working with fabric, beading, and photo transfer   82

Final Gallery   More Inspiration   100

Patterns   106

Resources   118

Contributors   120

About the Author   127

Acknowledgments   128

Introduction

"High is our calling, friend!
Creative art demands the service
of a mind and heart, though
sensitive, yet, in their weakest
part, heroically fashioned."

William Wordsworth

Creative doll making. These words are at the center of what defines us as doll makers. We are artists who have a passion to create. If others like or appreciate what we do, fine. If not, the love of what we do sustains us. As artists, we think outside the box, whereas others keep within what is familiar. There is no way to predict when our inspirations will come or where they will come from, but when they arrive, we frantically search for the nearest scratch pad.

This book is for people who know they have the gift of artistic creativity and want to take their doll-making talents to a higher level. It's also for those who have recently discovered a yearning to be creative—for those who never thought they could be doll makers. It's my hope that this book enables you to start with a published pattern and make a doll that's unique. I want to help you learn to create a doll that has your signature, a doll that is truly yours.

Being creative goes beyond scratch pads, needles, thread, sewing machines, and colored pencils. It begins when we rise in the morning. The creative person reflects their calling in the way they dress, cook, go to work, look at the world, interact with others, and think.

This is more than a book about doll making. I hope it will help you integrate creative techniques into many areas of your life—and allow you to take new risks, let go, and have fun! For example, rubber stamps and paints aren't new, but using them on already-made cloth figures is a fresh concept. Tyvek has been around for years, mainly for envelopes and environmental suits, but here you'll see how it can be used to create whimsical clothing and beads. And beading! What a wonderful art form. You'll see that when beads are used to embellish a cloth doll, your creation can become magical. Free-motion machine embroidery has been used to create wonderful garments for adults; you'll discover how to use it to change the look of fabric for doll clothing, shoes, wings, and bodices. Fabric collage is commonly found in quilting and garments, but it's also an exciting technique for making doll bodies and clothing.

This book contains patterns for three doll bodies and also for accessories. The doll pattern pieces are designed so that you can mix and match body parts as you wish. In each chapter, after the main doll project is introduced and described in detail, there is a gallery section where family, friends, and colleagues have interpreted the same patterns in their own style. You'll see the work of beginning doll makers, intermediate doll makers, and some "Hall of Fame" artists, too! This will give you lots of inspiration for making a doll that's uniquely yours.

This book is for you, the reader. I hope you enjoy reading each page as an adventure in creativity. Our world is one of heads, threads, beads, and the seeds of new ideas. I'm sure many of you will use the book to come up with new and exciting techniques. I hope you will share your creations with me and with others in the wonderful world of doll making. More than anything, I hope that you'll have fun.

Patti Culea

The Basics

Exploring key techniques

Art projects begin with basic techniques. Doll making is no different. An understanding and appreciation of those techniques will help in your creative process and enable you to take full advantage of the methods presented in each chapter.

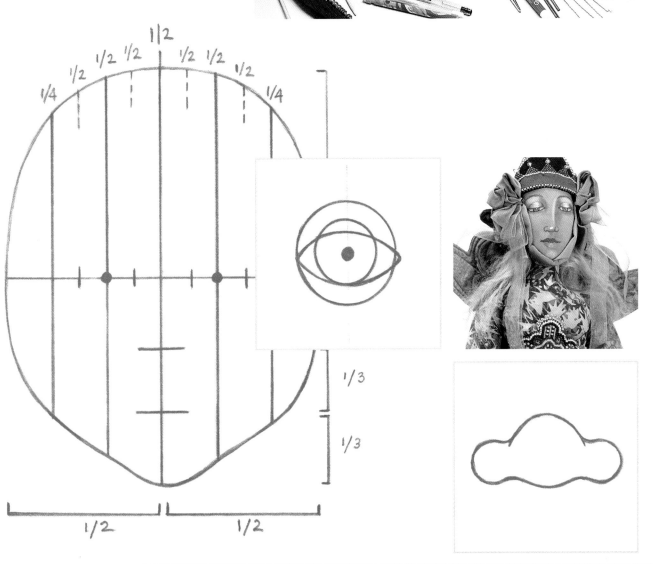

Gathering the Necessary Supplies

Doll making has changed dramatically over the past several years, with new techniques, supplies, and materials being discovered every day. Many supplies that doll makers use come from places like hardware stores and thrift shops; others come simply from the imaginations of the doll makers themselves.

Just as carpenters and plumbers have toolboxes to house and transport their essential tools, doll makers must have a basic sewing kit. You'll need it at home and, when you travel, to take to classes.

The Basic Kit

Work Space Essentials

Container for water

Containers for mixing dyes and paints

Cover-up or old clothes to wear

Fabric eraser

Hemostats—for turning and stuffing

Large and small finger-turning tools

Latex or plastic gloves

Measuring tape

Mechanical pencil

Paper towels

Plastic work surface

Sewing machine (your closest friend); cleaned and oiled and with a new needle

Sponges—small and large

Stuffing forks

Sweater rack for your clothes dryer or a hair dryer for setting paints and dyes

Cutting Tools

Paper and/or craft scissors

Pinking shears

Rotary cutter with extra blades

Rotary mat

Sharp scissors for cutting curves

Small scissors for cutting out fingers

Needles and Pins

Embroidery needles, tapestry needles (have one with the end of the eye cut off for making ribbon roses), a 3" (7.5 cm) doll-sculpting needle

Hand-sewing needles; long darning needles and/or quilter's basting needles

Machine needles—sharps in sizes 10, 12, metallic, embroidery, and topstitch

Needle threader with a cutter

Pincushion with straight pins

Safety pins

Threads

Decorative threads, such as metallic, rayon, and polyester threads

Good-quality polyester threads for your machine and hand sewing

Strong quilter's thread and/or upholstery thread for sculpting

Art Supplies

Colored pencils—preferably Prismacolor pencils (These work better on fabric than other brands.)

Gel Pens—white, black, red, colors of choice for eyes

Sulky's Ultra Solvy (a water-soluble stabilizer) or Craft Mistress Romeo (for those in the United Kingdom or "down under")

Zig Millennium pens in nib size 0.005, in brown, black, red; Micron Pigma Pens (Most other pens bleed on fabric.)

Body Supplies

High-quality cream- or white-colored pima cotton

Fairfield's Polyfil Stuffing

Pipe cleaners for wiring fingers

Hair Supplies

Felting needles

Mohair

Strips of fabric

Yarn

Dyeing and Painting Supplies

Colorhue Silk Dyes by Things Japanese

"Impress Me" rubber stamps by Sherrill Kahn

Jacquard's Dye-NA-Flow paints

Jacquard's Lumiere paints

Jacquard's Pearl-EX pigments

Jacquard's Textile paints

Margarita salt (available at grocery stores)

Rock salt

Wide round and flat brushes in sizes 10, 12, and 14

Special Effects Supplies

Beads—size 11 seed beads, accent beads

Fancy yarns for creating freeform clothing and embellishments

Silk caps—available at weaving stores

Laying Out Patterns

Before sewing any patterns in this book, look over the pattern pieces. Some have tracing and sewing lines, others have seam allowances. For the pieces that have tracing and sewing lines, trace onto the wrong side of the fabric, double the fabric, and sew. For the other patterns, either trace onto the wrong side of the fabric, double the fabric, and cut out, or make templates, trace, and cut out. Just remember to look at the pattern pieces before jumping in and sewing.

The head patterns have an arrow, which should be lined up with the grain of the fabric. The grain runs along the selvage of the fabric. The selvage is in line with the finished end of the fabric, not the cut end. This is important because it puts the stretch of the fabric where the cheeks are, so when you fill the doll's head with stuffing, it will have a nice plump face, rather than a long, skinny one.

1. Lay out the paper pattern on a table—a light table if you have one. Lay your fabric on top of the paper pattern, with the wrong side of fabric facing you. Using a mechanical pencil, trace all pattern pieces. Trace the darts, too. Double the fabric, and pin it in several places. For pattern pieces that don't have tracing and sewing lines, simply cut the pieces out. For those that have the lines, sew the pieces, and then cut them out.

2. For larger body parts and the legs, use pinking shears to cut them out to avoid the need to go around clipping curves. Avoid using pinking shears for the face and hands because these parts are too small.

3. When sewing the hands and face, use a shorter stitch length on your machine.

4. When sewing the doll's body parts, note the openings. These are important when putting the parts together and turning them right side out. Some pattern pieces have tabs that provide extra fabric for folding down so that it's easier to create a clean hand-sewn seam.

5. After sewing the body parts together, you'll turn the body parts right side out. (Note that the steps for doing this vary depending on the particular project.) Hemostats work well for this step, for everything but fingers. Reach in with the hemostats, grab the end of the foot, leg, or other body part and pull. Use the closed end of the hemostats to go back in and smooth out curves.

Turning Fingers

Although turning fingers does take practice, certain tools are available to make the process easier. You can buy an Itsy Bitsy Finger Turning kit created for doing just that (see Resources, page 118), or you can improvise and buy a couple of tubes from a hobby store that carries model train supplies. The tubes come in various widths; $1/16$", $3/32$", $5/32$", and $1/8$" (0.2 to 0.3 cm) are good for turning fingers. Just keep in mind that the tubes come in 12" (30.5 cm) lengths, so you'll need to cut them in half first.

If you're using the tubes, begin by inserting the largest tube inside a finger. Then, using the smallest tube, turn over the seam allowance, and push against the finger. Pull the finger up onto the smaller tube. The pressure against the seam allowance will help push the finger inside the hand.

You'll need two hands to do this, so hold the larger tube against your stomach. After you turn each finger, reach in with your hemostats, and turn the hand and then arm right side out.

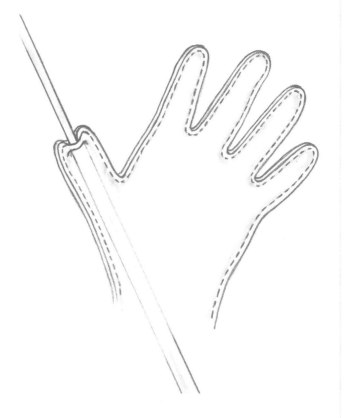

Begin by inserting
the largest tube inside a finger.

AUTHOR'S SUGGESTION

If this is your first time turning fingers this way, be patient. Although this step takes practice, it's worth learning because it helps prevent the seams at the fingers from bursting open. If they do, don't worry: That finger will determine which is your left or right hand because you'll use that side for the fingernail. More on that later.

Stuffing Body Parts

Use whichever stuffing you prefer, but avoid the type that feels like cotton because this type doesn't sculpt well. When stuffing body parts, except the hands, grab as much stuffing as you can to fit through the opening, and feed the stuffing into the part. Larger bunches of stuffing give a smooth look; smaller bunches, a lumpy look.

To stuff a body part, start by pushing the stuffing into the outside of the part first, and then fill up the inside. This technique helps prevent wrinkling. For small parts like the nose, place a small amount there, and then continue filling in with large amounts of stuffing.

When stuffing the hands, use a stuffing fork to place small amounts of stuffing in the fingers and then hemostats to fill up the hand and arm. (See Resources, page 118, for more information on stuffing forks.)

For a more realistic look, you can insert pipe cleaners into the fingers to give the appearance that the doll has bones in her hands. Pinch back both ends of all pipe cleaners. Bend four pipe cleaners in half, placing one end in one finger and the other end in the finger next to it, until every finger has a pipe cleaner. The pipe cleaners should be in line with each other. The two straight pipe cleaners are for the thumbs. Place these in the thumbs.

To complete the look, push the arm fabric down, and wrap the thumb pipe cleaner around the two bent ends of the pipe cleaners in the doll's fingers, allowing some of the pipe cleaner to stick up in the arm. If the fingers look like they need just a bit more stuffing, you can insert it now. Push back the fabric, and wrap the stuffing around the stuffing fork so it looks like a cotton swab, and then insert it into a finger. Next fill the palm side of each hand with stuffing, and continue filling up the arms around the pipe cleaner.

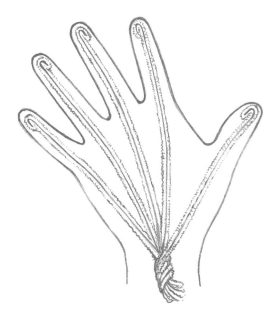

Wrap the thumb pipe cleaner around
the two bent ends of the pipe cleaners
in the doll's fingers.

Creating the Face

Most people find creating the face to be the most challenging—or even intimidating—task when it comes to doll making, but once you learn how to place features and find out which materials work best, you won't fear faces again. After all, you don't need to be an artist to create the face you want on a doll: You simply need to relax, have some fun, and let your creativity flow.

Human faces are designed perfectly for drawing because they're grafted out. For a doll's face, all that's needed are a few lines to create the foundation for the details.

1. To graft the face, start by drawing a line lengthwise down the center of the face with a mechanical pencil. (Note that you don't need to do this on the faces that have a seam down the center.)

2. Next, draw a line at the halfway point between the forehead and the chin.

3. Slice off about one-quarter at each side of the face.

4. Half each side of the face again. This creates the center for the eyes and outside corners of the mouth.

5. Halve each half again. This designates where the inside and outside corners of the eyes will be.

6. Below the half mark widthwise, split the rest of the face in thirds. This provides the basic graft for placing features. The rest of the features are made up of circles and ovals. For a male doll, use more squares than circles. The eyes are drawn first because most features are created from points on the eyes.

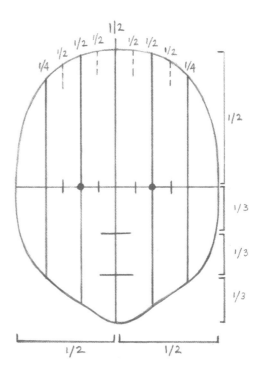

[step 6]
Below the half mark widthwise,
split the rest of the face in thirds.

AUTHOR'S SUGGESTION

If you're right-handed, draw the left side first; if you're left-handed, do the opposite. By drawing the weak side first, it's much easier to match the strong side. First, square off where you'll place the eyes, then just below the halfway line widthwise, place a line.

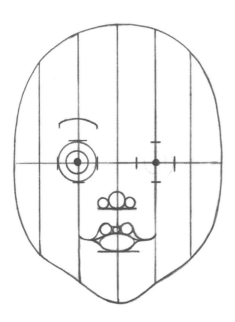

Now you can draw the eyes,
which are simply three circles.

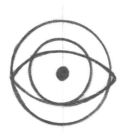

Next draw the upper eyelid.

The Eyes

Next measure the distance between the center line and each line on either side of that center line. This measurement determines the height and width of the eye. Faces should be 5 eye-widths wide, with 1 eye-width in between each eye. Grafting out the face helps guarantee the accuracy of this measurement. Now you can draw the eyes, which are simply three circles. The large circle, which fits inside the "box" that you created, becomes the eyeball. Inside that first circle is another circle, which represents the iris, or the colored part of the eye. Inside the second circle is the third and smallest circle, which represents the pupil.

Next draw the upper eyelid. Start at the inside corner of the eye at the halfway line. Curve the eyelid to touch the iris, and then continue the curve to the outside of the eyeball at the halfway mark. Depending on the look you're after, the lower lid can touch the iris or leave a bit of the eyeball showing.

The eyebrows are $\frac{1}{4}$" to $\frac{1}{3}$" (0.6 to 0.8 cm) above the eyes. They start straight up from the inside corner of the eye and extend to the outside corner. To achieve the full brow, draw a slightly curved line to connect these points.

The Nose

The nose is also made up of three circles. One large circle is drawn on the center line and above, but touching, the one-third line you drew when you split the face. On either side of the nose, keeping inside the one-quarter line, draw two smaller circles. Draw in the nostrils.

The Mouth

The mouth is made up of three circles, an oval, and wavy lines. First, draw two dots straight down from the pupils on the one-third line for the mouth. Draw a small circle at the center of the mouth. On either side of this circle draw larger circles, again keeping within the one-quarter line. Underneath these three circles draw an oval.

Draw a wavy line at the center of the mouth, starting at the milk bud and curving up and around the larger circles on either side. To finish the upper lip, start at the center and curve up and around the circles and down to the outside corners of the mouth. Follow the same sequence for the lower lip, referring to the illustration on the right as needed.

Stand back and look at the face, then make any necessary adjustments. Just keep in mind that slight variations are what make a doll's face unique, so don't get too focused on perfectly lining up the eyes when human eyes aren't perfectly aligned themselves. Because pencil marks will disappear when you color the face, you'll need to create a permanent outline. So once you're satisfied with the placement of the eyelids, irises, pupils, nostrils, and lips, outline them with a brown pen (for example, a Micron Pigma or Zig Millennium pen). After you've outlined everything, erase all pencil marks.

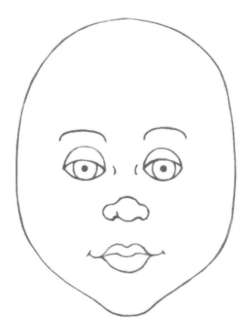

Each subsequent chapter includes additional details for coloring and sculpting the various doll faces. Although each face is different, the basic principles are referred to as each doll is explained. Also, notice how each doll maker in the Gallery sections interprets the basic patterns and techniques in each chapter. You'll see that the variation possibilities are endless!

Surfaces and Coloration

Working with dyes, paints, and stamps

One of the most exciting things you can do is create a beautiful painting from a blank canvas. In doll making, you essentially do the same thing— you transform a blank doll into a beautiful work of art.

This chapter takes you through the steps of making a beginning doll. After you sew her together, she becomes a blank canvas. You'll then embellish this canvas using dyes, paints, and stamps. You'll also learn more details about creating a face for your doll.

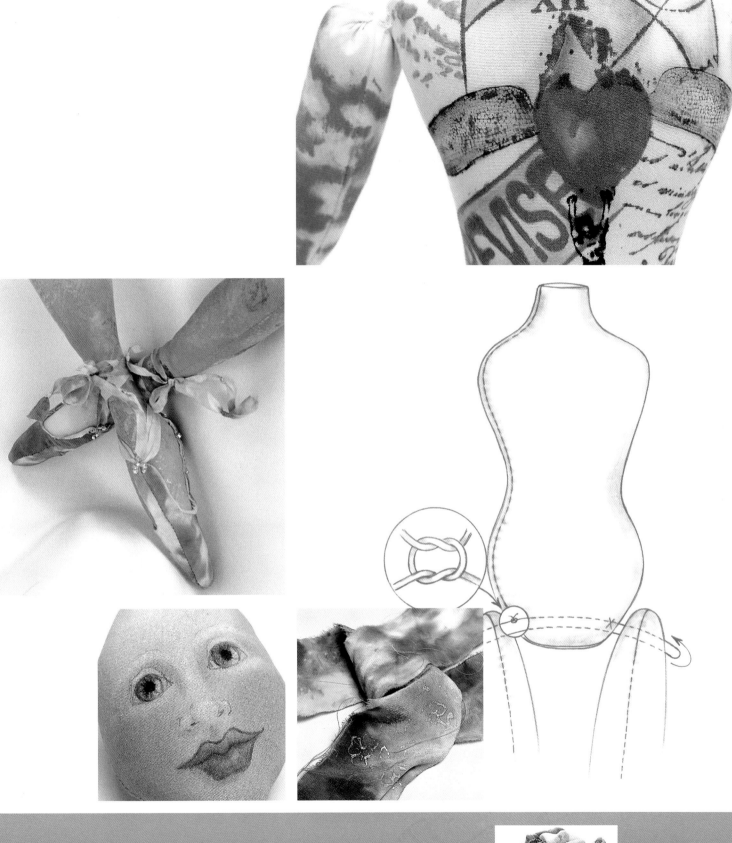

Beginning Doll

The doll featured in this chapter, Willamae (Doll #1), is a perfect project to start with if you're new to doll making. She's constructed from the pattern found on pages 106 and 107. The pattern is simple. Her head is flat, a perfect canvas for learning the basic principles for drawing a face. Her body is formed with only one pattern piece, and her hands and feet are simple silhouettes for easy sewing.

The first layer of design on this doll is a dyed surface. You'll learn to color the body, mixing several dyes to achieve a pretty flesh color, and then to embellish this layer with stamped designs. Feel free to adapt the palette to your liking as a way to start personalizing your design.

Her clothing is made from silk crepe de chine, which is also dyed and stamped. The simple torn pieces are draped into a lovely outfit and embellished with silk ribbons and ribbon roses. It's easy to transform simple scraps of fabric into fabulous garments by wrapping, gathering, and draping the pieces in interesting ways. If you feel ambitious, you can even add shoes to the ensemble, or go without. It's up to you.

Finally, you'll learn, step-by-step, how to continue to add detail to your doll's face, using pencils, gel pens, and rubber stamps.

Supplies

$^1/_4$ yard (23 cm) pima cotton

pins

thread to match

scissors

mechanical pencil and soft eraser

stuffing

stuffing tools

hemostats

hand-sewing needles

strong thread for attaching the head, arms, and legs

3" (7.5 cm) needle to attach legs

fabric marking pens: brown, red, black

plastic bag to cover workspace

paper towel

ice cube tray

Jacquard's Dye-NA-Flow paints: white, ecru, ochre, magenta, sun yellow, turquoise

Jacquard's Lumiere paints: super sparkle, silver, turquoise

paper plate and sponge

rubber stamps

$^1/_4$ yard (23 cm) silk crepe de chine

eye droppers

3 yards (2.7 m) 7-mm white silk ribbon

matches and a candle

pie plate with water (optional)

beads

colored pencils: sienna brown, cream, white, carmine red, periwinkle, peacock blue, copenhagen blue, scarlet lake

gel pens: black, purple, white

glitzy yarns

[step 4]
Cut a slit on one side of the
head toward the chin.

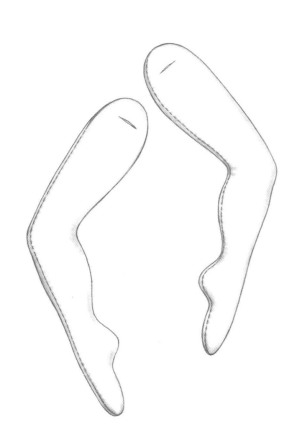

[step 5]
Cut slits toward the top of each leg.

Making the Body

1. Arrange and trace the patterns for Doll #1 onto the wrong side of the body fabric. (See Chapter 1, page 14.) Then double the fabric, right sides together, and pin in several places.

2. Begin sewing the body parts together, leaving a section open, for turning, as indicated on the patterns. *Note:* The head and legs don't have openings; you'll cut a slit later for turning. When sewing the neck, backstitch at the beginning, and then double stitch just the neck sides. This will prevent the seams from busting out.

3. Cut out all body pieces.

4. Cut a slit on one side of the head toward the chin. Make this slit on the side of the head with pencil marks.

5. Cut slits toward the top of each leg. Make sure you have a right leg and a left leg by placing the legs together and positioning the slits on adjacent sides.

6. Turn all pieces, right sides out.

7. This step is optional, but it gives the finished doll a nice look: Follow the markings on the hand template to trace in fingers on the hands and topstitch by machine. Do this before filling up the doll body with stuffing. When topstitching, do a backstitch at the beginning and end of each finger, to keep any threads from coming loose while stuffing.

8. Use the stuffing to fill the main body first. Fill the doll until it feels firm, especially the neck. Fill the head next. Smooth out any wrinkles in the fabric by filling with more stuffing.

[step 7]
Follow the markings on the hand template to trace in fingers on the hands and topstitch by machine.

9. Place the head on the neck by grabbing the neck with your hemostats and pushing it up into the opening at the back of the head. Pin in place. Thread a regular hand-sewing needle with ¼-yard (46 cm) of strong thread. Place a knot in the end. Ladder stitch the head to the neck. Anchor the thread at the back of the head, and cut.

10. Stuff the legs. After the legs are filled, ladder stitch the openings closed with a needle and thread.

11. Thread a 3" (7.5 cm) needle with 2 yards (1.8 m) of strong thread. Put a knot in the end of the thread, and attach to the side of the hip.

12. Place the leg at the hip, and attach by running a threaded needle through the leg. Go back through the leg, over to the other side, and through the other leg. Go back and forth at least three times, then anchor the thread at the inside of the hip (under a leg).

13. Fill the arms with stuffing, starting with the fingers, using the stuffing fork. Finish filling the arms with stuffing to ¼" (0.6 cm) below the opening. Sew a gathering stitch along the top of each arm. Push the raw edges of the fabric inside as you do this. Tack the arm to the side of the body at the shoulders with a stitch.

14. Repeat for the other arm. The doll is now ready to be dyed, stamped, and clothed.

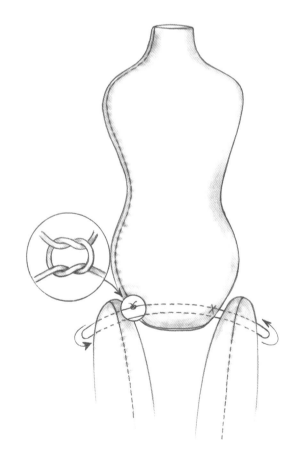

[step 11]
Put a knot in the end of the thread, and attach to the side of the hip.

Drawing the Face

Before dyeing, draw in the facial features. (See "Drawing Faces," pages 17 to 19.) Outline all drawn features with a brown fabric marking pen.

Adding Color with Dye

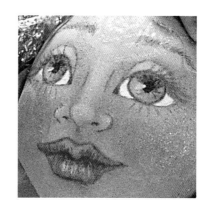

Jacquard's Dye-NA-Flow paints dye just about any fiber but polyester. When used straight from the container, they keep their color; however, when diluted, they do fade a bit. They don't change the "hand," or feel, of the fabric. They're also nontoxic; therefore, they don't have harmful fumes or much of an odor, so it's unnecessary to wear goggles or a mask when using them.

These paints should be heat set—and, fortunately, that's quite simple to do. If you have a sweater rack for your clothes dryer, set the dryer for cotton, place the dyed doll body on the rack, and dry for 30 minutes. If you don't have a sweater rack, use your hair dryer or a heat gun (found at stamp stores and hardware stores). You can also use an iron to set the colors. When dyeing a doll that isn't going to be laundered, heat setting is unnecessary. Heat setting simply guarantees that the colors won't fade.

To set up a dye space, gather an ice cube tray, some brushes, a container for water, paper towels, and a plastic garbage bag.

1. Lay down the plastic bag to cover the workspace. Next put a layer of paper towels on top of the plastic. The towels will catch any spills and are good for dabbing the brush on when doing some of the dry-brush techniques.

2. Pour a teaspoon of each dye into the different sections of the ice cube tray. Leave a few sections empty for mixing colors together.

3. To create a flesh color, add 1 teaspoon of white, then add a drop at a time of ecru and ochre until you get the shade of flesh you want. Add a drop of magenta to this mixture and a little sun yellow. If the color is too dark, add a bit of water and more white.

4. Brush this mixture onto the flesh parts of the doll body. Working quickly, add other colors, as desired, to cover the entire body. Work quickly because the dyes dry fast, and if you go back and paint next to a dry spot, it will produce a watermark.

5. For cheek color, place a small amount of a skin-toned dye in an empty space of the ice cube tray, and add some magenta. Pick up a small amount of dye on your brush, and dab onto a paper towel to remove excess. Brush her cheeks with this color. The color should bleed.

Any stamp will work on cloth. Intricate stamps are my favorites, such as "Impress Me" stamps by Sherrill Kahn. Because the stamps aren't mounted onto a hard surface, it's easy to bend the stamp around a small arm or other curved parts of the body.

Adding Interest with Stamps

When working with stamps, dab on just a bit of the paint with a sponge. Pick up some paint on the sponge, then dab off any extra paint onto your pallet, thus enabling you to put just the right amount of paint onto the stamp. Have water and an old toothbrush handy; the paints dry quickly and can ruin the stamps if not cleaned as soon as you finish stamping.

Experiment with several colors of paint on a stamp. The colors will bleed together to create other colors. For instance, yellow and blue will make green where the two colors meet, creating some interesting effects.

1. Using the Lumiere paints, place a dollop of each color onto a paper plate. Pick up some paint on a sponge, and dab onto a stamp. Immediately stamp the doll's body. Continue this stamping process until you have the effect you want.

2. Let the paints dry thoroughly. Set an iron to the cotton setting. Set the paints by lightly ironing over the body parts.

Making Clothes

Use silk or cotton for clothing. In the featured doll, silk crepe de chine is used.

1. Wet a piece of the silk crepe de chine thoroughly with plain tap water. Squeeze out excess water.

2. Place small amounts of sun yellow, turquoise, and magenta into the ice cube tray that you used earlier. Scrunch up the silk, and dip into the yellow. With eye droppers, drop magenta and turquoise onto the remaining white areas of the silk. Squeeze out excess dye, and hang the fabric up to dry. Let the colors set for 24 hours, then iron the silk with a warm iron.

3. Using the eye dropper technique only, color the silk ribbons. Ribbons are much narrower than the fabric, so the piece could get too saturated by dipping it into one color first.

Dye-NA-Flow paints will work beautifully on the silk, or you can use any silk dye. Some silk dyes need to be steam set, so be sure to check the manufacturer's labels.

4. Once the fabric is dry, measure the doll's body, and decide how long you want her skirt to be. Tear the fabric to the desired length. (The featured doll's skirt measures 18" x 4" [45.5 x 10 cm]). Light a candle, and carefully run the torn edge along the flame to seal the edge.

5. Using the Lumiere paints and stamps, create designs on the silk. The silk can be stamped before or after it's dyed.

6. For the bodice, tear two strips of fabric 10" x 1½" (25.5 x 4 cm). Wrap these two around each other as shown below.

[step 6]
Wrap these two strips
around each other.

7. Bring one side up over her shoulders and the other side around to her back. With a needle and thread, tack in place at the back. On one shoulder, tear a long strip of silk, 10" x ½" (25.5 x 1.3 cm), and tie it in various places. Then loop the strip, and tack it to her shoulder. Create some silk ribbon roses or other flowers, and sew these to her bodice. (See the photo on page 23 for ideas.)

8. Her skirt is one long strip of fabric, 18" x 4" (45.5 x 10 cm). With right sides together, sew up the back seam, along the 4" (10 cm) edges. Then gather the waist by hand with a running stitch. Slip the skirt onto her body, and pull the threads to fit the waist. Tack in place.

9. The upper skirt is another strip of fabric, 18" x 4" (45.5 x 10 cm), folded over to create a double ruffle. Hand-gather at the center, and pull the threads to fit at the waist. Leave open at the center.

10. Stamp on her body and her clothing. Add some silk ribbons at her waist and a silk ribbon rose.

Adding Shoes

1. Trace four shoe patterns onto the wrong side of the silk scrap (left over from the skirt and top). Two are for the outside of the shoes, and two are for the lining. Double the fabric, and sew along the solid line, leaving open where marked.

2. Cut out all pieces, and turn two of them right side out. Place the two lining pieces inside the other two, and pin in place with right sides together. Sew along the raw edges from the back of the shoe all the way around. To turn the shoes right side out, cut a slit in the lining at the bottom in the seam, then turn right side out. Finger-press along edges, and slip the shoes onto her feet.

3. Fold a 12" (30.5 cm) length of silk ribbon in half, and tack at the center of the top of the shoe. Bring the ribbon to the back of the shoe, and tack in place. Wrap the ribbons around her ankles as shown in the photo on page 23, then tie in front, just above her ankle, in a bow. Tack in place. Hide the knot under the shoe top. Add some beads at the center top of shoe where the silk ribbon is attached.

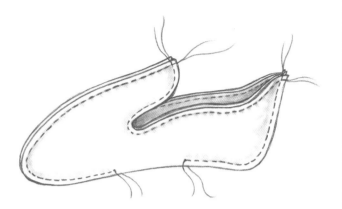

[step 1]
Double the fabric, and sew along the
solid line, leaving open where marked.

AUTHOR'S SUGGESTION

The shoes are an optional embellishment. Some of the artists who made dolls from this pattern chose not to make shoes; others did.

Finishing the Face

1. Assemble colored pencils, gel pens, and fabric pens.

2. Start by shading the various parts of the face. Using the sienna brown pencil, start by shading the temple, above the eye crease, down the sides of the nose, under her nose, in the upper lip, down one side of the lower lip, and under the lower lip.

3. With the cream pencil, color in next to the brown. The face will start to curve upward and catch light. The cream creates this effect on a flat-faced doll. Use the cream to color just a bit under each eye and along her upper lip.

4. Using the white pencil, lighten the forehead, the center of the nose, across the ball of the nose and each flare, and the center of the chin. Before blending, brighten up her cheeks with the carmine red pencil.

5. Blend all of this pencil work with a scrap of fabric.

The Lips

1. The lips use two shades of red. Color in both upper and lower lips with carmine red, then use scarlet lake to darken the upper lip and down one side of the lower lip. Darken a bit of the lower lip along the bottom edge.

2. Lighten the center of her lower lip with the white pencil. Outline both upper and lower lips with the red gel roller or fabric pen. Use a brown fabric pen to outline the center of her lips.

The Eyes

The eyes can be created using three shades of one color or three different colors. For this doll, three different blues are used—periwinkle, peacock blue, and copenhagen blue.

1. Using the lightest shade first, fill in the irises. To evoke light hitting the doll's face from her left, make that side of her eyes lighter. Using the medium shade, color in under her upper eyelid and down the side of the eye that's in the shadow. Using the darkest shade, color in just under the eyelid. With the white pencil, lighten the side of the eye that's catching the light.

2. Blacken the pupils with the black gel roller. Outline the irises with the purple gel roller, and run some spokes out from the pupils.

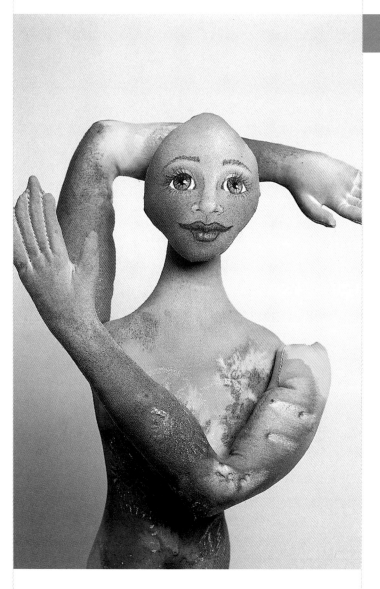

Finishing the Doll

1. Color in the whites of her eyes with the white gel roller. Add a highlight to each pupil on the side that's catching the light. Place a dot of red with a fabric pen or red pencil at the inside corners of each eye to represent the tear duct.

2. Outline her eyelids with the brown fabric pen again. Feather in her eyelashes: Start at the center above the pupil, and draw a short eyelash and then a long one, and alternate between adding a short lash and a long one until you have a pleasing effect. Her lower eyelashes will be shorter and lighter in color. Draw them in with a light touch.

3. The eyebrows are feathered in following the line you drew at the beginning. Always start with the brown pen, and change to black if you feel she needs darker eyebrows and eyelashes.

4. Outline her nostrils and the flare of her nose. Add some more shading and highlights if you feel she needs it. Add eye shadow with other colors.

5. Finish the face with more stamps.

6. For the head piece, loop silk scraps and tack them along her hairline (seam line), and fill in the bald spots with more silk loops. Add a silk ribbon and some glitzy yarns.

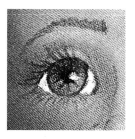

Senta's Baggage

ARTIST: Claudia Medaris   (Pattern: Doll #1)

"Senta's Baggage is a rubber-stamped doll. Any rubber stamp is suitable with fabric paints, though larger stamps, or ones with fewer details, tend to make a cleaner image on fabric. I suggest you work with tightly woven fabrics and clean the stamps carefully after each use.

I coordinated the primary rubber images for this piece with various larger background stamps. Using fabric paint, stamp dabbers, and masking techniques, I embellished the entire surface of the cloth doll with an array of connecting images. I then inked the main foreground stamp with hues of fabric paint. While wet, these paints blend easily when you dab them on the surface of the rubber image."

Pattielise

ARTIST: elinor peace bailey   (Pattern: Doll #1)

"This doll uses a slightly modified version of the Beginner pattern. I used an embellishment technique I learned from Elise Peeples which uses Liquatex Gel Medium, crocheted lace, Gesso and Jacquard paints and dyes. I thought I would call the doll Pattielise. She is organic and seems to grow new horns at every turn in the bend.

It was fun not to have the road mapped out too clearly. Patti, Elise, and I have been making dolls for years, and we were bound to rub off on one another from time to time. This doll shows this with the influence of Patti's dyeing and Elise's collage with a bit of my own drawings and colors thrown in."

Culeoptera

ARTIST: Barbara Chapman (Pattern: Doll #2)

"I began by painting Culeoptera's body with a generous coating of Gesso, but then smoke fairies descended overnight and smeared a layer of charcoal on her body. [*Author's note*: This charcoal effect was from a recent house fire that destroyed much of the artist's beautiful artwork.] Luckily the Gesso layer prevented most of the smoke from seeping through. I then painted her with Jacquard's Dye-NA-Flow paints, which, of course, wouldn't penetrate the fabric in a dyelike fashion because of the Gesso. On parts of her body and face, I used Lumiere metallic paints.

In dressing her, I wanted to show some of the body, so I loosely crocheted a sweater for her and paired it with snazzy handmade felt pants with velvet cuffs. I created jazzy metallic stockings by needle weaving down to the velvet-and-gold-encrusted shoes. I added layers of sleeves, collaging surfaces over each other to create an interesting effect. I collaged some sheer lace and calligraphy papers to her face to create a contemporary fantasy feel and to tie in with the textures in the costume.

Culeoptera was a work in progress. Trial and error with painted leather, needle-woven stockings, and hair styles took her through several identity crises, but everything came together with antique sari border sequins and gilding. With hair wound with lace from India, a few collage elements, and embellishments, she was done. I named my doll Culeoptera in honor of Patti Culea, who brought about her metamorphosis."

Irulan

ARTIST: Janet Beth Cruz   (Pattern: Doll #2)

"To start Irulan, I looked through fashion magazines like *Harper's Bazaar* and *Vogue* to find a stylish outfit for my retro doll. Then I focused on the colors. It's always fun to use bright colors, colors that you love but never find yourself wearing or using in your home. For me, it's bright pinks, reds, oranges, and yellows. When I was ready to dye her body, I used Jacquard's Dye-NA-Flow paints—sun yellow, scarlet, bright orange, and hot fuchsia. For her face I used their salmon, ochre, and white. Although you don't see much of her body, it's just as bright as her outfit.

Her shoes were a dilemma. I knew what I wanted but wasn't sure how to achieve it. I finally drew the design on paper. With help from my mom, Patti Medaris Culea, we added seam allowances, and I was ready to make them from fabric. After sewing and stuffing the shoes, I attached them to her feet and embellished them with beads. Irulan carries a hand-dyed purse and lounges on three beanbags. She's ready to pose for any photo shoot."

Leading by a Hare

ARTIST: Margaret (Marge) Clok Gorman   (Pattern: Doll #3)

"On the day Patti's pattern arrived, I set my imagination loose to make a doll with no limits for painting, stamping, or dying techniques. I had a hare-brained idea: I wanted the doll to be a rabbit with human characteristics. As I began construction, I chose not to incorporate the moveable joints provided in the pattern and instead ladder stitched the arms and legs for a fully posed doll. I eliminated the bust, and I added ears and a fluffy tail.

My idea was to dye all the body parts except the head and hands. I saturated both sides of the doll from the neck to the feet with a spray bottle filled with water. Next came Jacquard's Dye-NA-Flow paints in green, blue, and purple. I dipped a toothbrush into the purple and spattered it all over the doll. I used the spray bottle again and got an exciting watercolor effect. I repeated the process with red, yellow, and orange. With the fabric still wet, I applied a bit of Jacquard Metallic bronze paint. After an overnight of drying, the colors became lighter.

The head is needle sculpted from penne velvet. The ears are painted with metallic white paint and a small amount of blushing. To create the eyelids and mouth, I sculpted penne velvet and formed them with tacky glue. His whiskers are silk threads and wire that are curled around a bamboo skewer. I painted his driving gloves with bronze metallic paint and cut out holes for the knuckles; I used black metallic paint to create stitching lines.

The steering wheel is 15-gauge wire, wrapped with stiffened fabric and then painted. I made the carrot car out of muslin, dying the body orange, red, yellow, and green and the wheels black. I used a carrot stamp to create the spokes. His shoes also have wheels to help him around 'harepin' curves. Once my rabbit had gloves, I had my doll's theme. Now I just do my best to keep him under 65 m.p.h."

Fabrications

Working with Tyvek, liners, and machine embroidery

After coloring a blank canvas, it's time to move on and embellish it. This chapter explores how to use free-motion machine embroidery, Tyvek, bonding sheets, diaper liners, silk ribbon work, needle lace, the button hole stitch, knitting, and crochet to embellish your doll. Some of the fabrications you'll be familiar with, others you won't. The important thing to remember is that they all create beautiful effects and are great fun—you simply need to experiment with them to find which ones are your favorites.

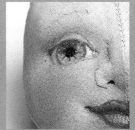

Intermediate Doll

Supplies for the Body

$^1/_3$ yard (30.5 cm) pima cotton

good-quality polyester thread

pins

scissors

stuffing

stuffing tools

pipe cleaners

long darning needle and strong thread

hemostats

hand-sewing needles

art supplies

two 25-mm wooden beads for legs

two 20-mm wooden beads for arms

paints and brushes

For this project, you'll use the second, intermediate doll pattern. This pattern has a bit more detail. The additional pattern pieces add more shape to the face and body. The doll becomes more like a puzzle, with you piecing the parts together to create a new look. This pattern introduces joints, which you can embellish. You'll create some articulated fingers. Even the foot starts to take on a more realistic shape.

Which fabric should you choose for her body? To give your doll a realistic look, you can make her from a flesh-colored fabric. Or you can dye the fabric after you've made the body, as explained in the previous chapter. To create a more fanciful look, you might consider using a batik fabric. Any type of fabric can be used to make a body— just make sure it has a tight weave and doesn't fray easily.

Arien, the sample doll (Doll #2), was created using a tightly woven pimatex cotton, which was then dyed. In this chapter, you'll discover many ways to embellish your doll's body and clothing. And because the face on this doll has greater dimension, you'll learn how to sculpt it to add even more detail.

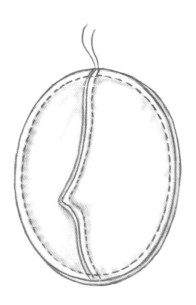

[step 3]
Sew all the way around.

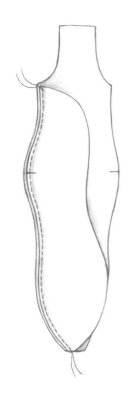

[step 5]
Sew from the center of the bust up
to the shoulder, then from the center of the
bust down to the bottom of the body.

Making the Body

1. Arrange and trace all patterns for Doll #2 onto the wrong side of the body fabric. (See Chapter 1, page 14.) Note those pattern pieces that have a seam allowance and those that don't.

2. Keep in mind that when doing the face and hands, you'll want to use a shorter stitch length on your sewing machine. Sew seam #1 on the Face and seam #2 on the Head Back, leaving open where marked. Cut out the two pieces. Open them up, and with right sides together, pin at the top of the head and at the chin.

3. Sew all the way around. Turn through the opening on the Head Back, and fill with enough stuffing so that the head is firm.

4. Sew seam #3 on the Body Back, leaving open where marked. Cut out all body pieces. (Keep in mind that if you use pinking shears, you won't have to clip curves.)

5. Matching the marks at the center of the bust, pin the Center Body Front to one Side Body Front piece. Sew from the center of the bust up to the shoulder, then from the center of the bust down to the bottom of the body.

   Do the same to the other Side Body Front piece. You now have a full body front.

6. Pin the Body Back to the full body front, and sew from the neck opening down the body and around up to the other side of the neck opening. Be sure to start out with a back stitch at the neck.

7. Turn the body right side out. Fill with enough stuffing so the body is firm. Be sure to plump up her breasts.

8. To stabilize the neck, place a pipe cleaner in it, but allow a bit of it to stick out so the head can rest on it. Close up the opening in the back with a ladder stitch, starting at the bottom of the opening and sewing up toward the top. When doing this, thread a long darning needle with about 1½ yards (1.5 m) of strong thread.

9. Attach the head to the neck by grabbing the neck with hemostats and pushing the neck into the opening at back of head. Ladder stitch the head to the neck.

10. Turning to the legs, sew from the opening at the knee all the way down to the opening at the toes on both sides of the Lower Leg. Cut out.

11. Fold the Lower Legs at the knees so the seams match. Sew along each tab, stopping short of the matched seams to leave an opening at the center.

12. For the feet, draw in a nice curve, as shown, and then sew, following your drawing.

13. Turn the Lower Leg through the opening at the top, and fill with stuffing. Close up the opening using a needle and thread.

14. The Upper Leg is sewn from the opening at the knee around the curve at the top and down to the other side of the opening.

15. Cut out the Upper Leg, fold at the knee, so the seams match. Sew along each tab, stopping short of the matched seam. Turn, and fill with stuffing. Close up the opening using a needle and thread.

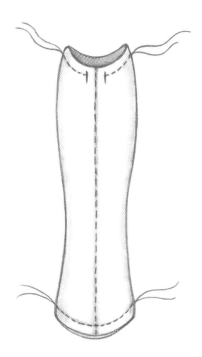

[step 11]
Sew tabs down to the center,
leaving them open at the center.

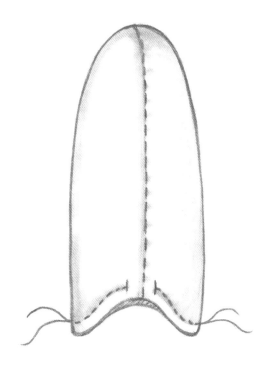

[step 15]
Close up the opening using
a needle and thread.

[step 16]
Join the Upper Leg to the
Lower Leg, using the beads.

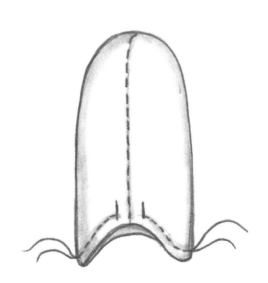

[step 19]
Fold the opening at the elbow
so the seams match. Sew across the tabs,
leaving it open at the center.

16. Paint the two 25-mm beads. After they're dry, join the Upper Leg to the Lower Leg, using the beads:

a. Thread a needle with about ½ yard (46 cm) of strong thread, and knot the end. Insert the needle at the end of one tab on the Upper Leg.

b. Go through the bead and into the other side of the tab. Go through the tab and back through the bead to the other side. Do this three times.

c. If you have enough thread, you can pick up the Lower Leg and do the same thing you did with the Upper Leg. You now have one full leg.

d. Do the same with the other leg.

17. After your legs are done, attach them to the body, using about 1 yard (91.5 cm) of strong thread and a long needle. Follow the instructions in Chapter 2, page 25, on how to do this.

18. Turning to the arms, sew the Upper Arm from the opening at the elbow around to the other side of the opening. Then cut it out.

19. Fold the opening at the elbow so the seams match. Sew across the tabs, leaving it open at the center. Turn the arm right side out, and fill it with stuffing.

20. Sew the Lower Arm from the opening at the elbow all the way around the fingers and back up to the other side of the opening at the elbow. When sewing around the fingers, be sure to have two stitches across the tips and two stitches in between the fingers. (There are two fingers attached. Don't sew down the dashed lines yet.)

21. Cut out the Lower Arm, clipping in between the fingers and at the curves around the wrist. When clipping between the fingers, clip at each side and right up to the stitches, to help prevent wrinkling once the hands are turned.

22. Fold the arm at the elbow as you did with the Upper Arm, and sew across the tabs, leaving it open at the center.

23. To turn the fingers, use either your favorite turning tool or the tubes described in Chapter 1, page 15.

24. After you turn the fingers, topstitch down the center of the two fingers that are attached. Finish the hands as described in Chapter 2, page 24.

25. Attach the arms to the 20-mm beads as you did with the legs, and attach the arms to the body as you did with the legs.

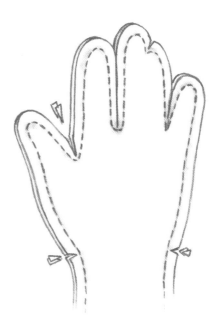

[step 20]
There are two fingers attached.
Don't sew down the dashed lines yet.

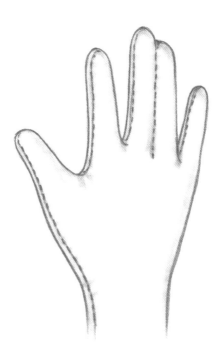

[step 24]
After you turn the fingers, topstitch down
the center of the two fingers that are attached.

Creating the Face

Follow the instructions in Chapter 1, pages 17 to 19, for grafting out and completing the face. (Because this doll has a center seam down her face, you don't have to worry about splitting it in half lengthwise.)

The photo below illustrates how the doll's face should be grafted. The left side shows more of the grafting and the right side the finished look. Once you outline your features with a brown fabric pen, you can erase all pencil marks.

Sculpting

Before coloring the doll's face, you'll want to sculpt it, using a needle and thread. As you go from one area to another, pull on your thread. However, look at the doll's face as you pull, because you don't want to pull so tight that you cause wrinkling—you simply want to define the features. Follow the steps below to work your way around the face:

1. Thread a long darning needle with 1 yard (91.5 m) of strong thread. The thread should be in a single strand, not doubled. Anchor this at the back of the doll's head.

2. Push the needle through the head and out the inside corner of an eye (**#1**).

3. Push the needle back inside the head at the corner of the eye and come out at the opposite nostril (**#2**).

4. Push the needle back inside the head at the nostril and come out at the opposite flare of the nose (**#3**).

5. Push the needle back inside at the flare and come out straight across at the opposite flare (**#4**).

6. Push the needle back inside at the flare and come out at the opposite nostril (**#5**).

7. Push the needle back inside at the nostril and come out at the opposite inside corner of the eye (**#6**).

8. Push the needle back inside at the corner of the eye and come out at the outside corner of the mouth (**#7**).

9. Push the needle back inside at the outside corner of the mouth and come out at the outside corner of the eye (**#8**).

10. Push the needle back inside at the outside corner of the eye and come out at the inside corner of the other eye (**#1**).

11. Push the needle back inside at the inside corner of the eye and come out at the outside corner of the mouth (**#9**).

12. Push the needle back inside at the outside corner of the mouth and come out at the outside corner of the eye (**#10**).

13. Push the needle back inside at the corner of the eye and come out at the back of the head, then anchor off.

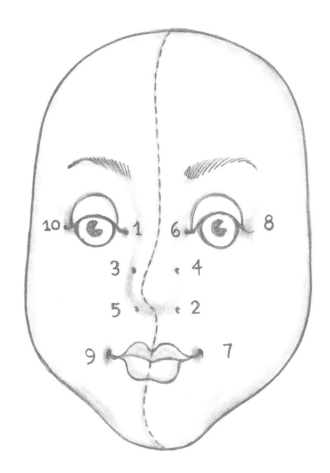

Numbers on the above face correspond to the bold numbers in the text on the left.

Adding Color

To color the face, follow the steps laid out in Chapter 2, page 26. Add shadows and highlights using the colored pencils.

Then color the eyes and lips with the colored pencils. Outline everything with the fabric pens, and add your highlights to the eyes with the white gel roller. The side-by-side comparison in the photos on the left show you the before and after.

Color in the irises with the lightest shade, then use the medium shade under the eyelid and down the side that is in the shadow. Use the darkest shade for under the upper eyelid.

After you finish the doll's face, set it with heat, using an iron.

Supplies for the Embellishments

¹/₄ yard (23 cm) velvet for skirt

wood block or rubber stamp

iron

diaper liner (Gerber EZ-liner) or disposable diaper

crayons

baking parchment

rayon and metallic sewing threads

³/₈"(0.9 cm) silk ribbon

doilies

needle and thread

¹/₄ yard (23 cm) silk chiffon

dye

double-sided bonding sheet

glitzy yarns and threads

hot air gun

strong water-soluble stabilizer

fabric-weight and medium-weight Tyvek

acrylic or fabric paint or markers

wooden barbecue skewers

¹/₄" (0.6 cm) washers

tapestry needle

size 4 knitting needles

size D crochet hook

aluminum foil

darning or free-motion foot

beading wire

Embellishing the Doll

Clothing and embellishing the doll is the fun part. There are so many new techniques and ideas available. In this section we'll explore several. The dolls in the Gallery section that follows include all of the techniques discussed in this chapter, making them a great source of inspiration.

Transferring Colors and Images

Along with a few basic supplies, a diaper liner can help you transfer color and images onto your doll's skirt in no time at all. If you can't find a box of diaper liners and you don't have a box of disposable diapers handy, ask a friend, relative, or neighbor who does. All it takes is one diaper liner. (Disposable diapers have a lining inside that's the same as the EZ-liners.)

The skirt needs to be done first because it's attached first. Cut a 20" x 8" (51 x 20.5 cm) piece from the 1/4 yard (23 cm) of velvet. Lay it down on an ironing board, velvet side up.

If you have a wood block, that will work best. (If you don't, use a large rubber stamp.) Lay the diaper liner on top of the wood block. Pick out the color of crayon you want, and rub it on the diaper liner. You'll see the design transfer to the liner. Then lay the diaper liner on top of the velvet, crayon side up. Lay a piece of baking parchment on top, and iron over the design area with the iron on the highest setting. Hold the iron in place for about 10 seconds, then move to the next area. Lift up the baking parchment to ensure that the image transfers. Some irons aren't as hot as others, so you may have to go over the image again.

The diaper liner melts into the velvet, leaving the design from your rubbing. Although this technique can be used on other fabrics, it works best on velvet. Also, some people recommend grease markers (Shiva Markers), but crayons seem to work far better. Plus they're easy to find, and they're inexpensive. You'll go through a crayon very quickly, depending on how large a design you want.

Using Free-Motion Machine Embroidery

Sewing-machine embroidery can add your unique mark of creativity to almost anything you make. It is fun, easy, and faster than hand embroidery. Almost any thread will work if the sewing machine is properly adjusted. Experiment to find threads that work best with your machine. Correct thread tension is very important. Usually, the top tension needs to be looser than the bottom. Adjust the machine to allow the bottom tension to pull the top thread down even with the underside of the material. It should not be loose enough to cause loops on the wrong side of your work.

To prepare the machine, remove the presser foot, put on a darning or free motion foot, and lower the feed dog. (On some machines, a lever may raise the throat plate to keep the feed dog from interfering with stitching.) Then, set the machine stitch length and width controls on "0". Always test the stitch tension and setting before beginning your project.

To begin stitching, use the hand-wheel, insert the needle into the fabric, and bring up the bobbin thread. Holding threads taut, take three or four small stitches to lock the threads in place. Clip off the loose thread ends. Continue stitching following any of these basic movements: moving vertically or horizontally, back and forth across the fabric, or moving in small circular or swirl patterns. The movements can form distinct rows of stitches, as shown in the skirt design that follows, or they may be blended by overlapping. To end stitching, move the stitch width regulator to "0". Then, stitch three or four stitches in the same place. Pull the threads to the wrong side, and clip close to the fabric. You can also combine or overlap straight stitches and zigzag stitches.

Adding Ribbons, Silk Strips, and Lace

Once you add a splash of color to your doll's skirt, you can embellish it even more using a few basic techniques. The sample doll skirt here used free-motion machine embroidery, silk ribbons, lace motifs (from an old doily), and torn silk strips to add interest.

Start by placing some variegated rayon thread in your machine and any thread in the bobbin. (The thread in the bobbin won't show.) Starting at the top of the fabric, stitch up and down the length of the skirt. When you're ready to add a silk ribbon or torn silk strip, start at the top and gather the ribbon or strip as illustrated. Continue down the length of the skirt. You can add some strips at the bottom of the skirt and bunch them up tighter.

To add a lace motif, position a doily on the skirt wherever you want that design, and then top-stitch it in place.

Finishing the Skirt

Once you have your skirt the way you want it, sew up the back seam and sew in a hem. (If you like, you can use decorative stitching for this.) Then sew a running stitch along the waist. Slip the skirt on the body and pull the threads at the waist to fit. Secure the threads by tying in an overhand knot then tack skirt to waist using a needle and thread.

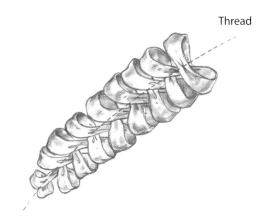

Thread

When you're ready to add a silk ribbon or torn silk strip, start at the top and gather the ribbon or strip.

53

Adding Glitz to the Bodice

Although the following technique happened by accident, it added glitz to the bodice just beautifully. To begin, tear two 10" x 4" (25.5 x 10 cm) pieces of silk chiffon. Dye them to match the doll's color scheme. As they dry (they'll do so fairly quickly), cut two pieces of double-sided bonding sheet the same size. Peel off the backing on one side of one sheet, and lay the sheet down on an ironing board, sticky side up. Throw bits and pieces of glitzy yarns and threads onto the sheet. Peel off the backing on one side of the second sheet, and lay this on top of your glitzy layer. With your iron on the highest setting, iron the two sheets together, creating a sandwich of glitz.

Set the sandwich aside, and lay down a piece of baking parchment on the ironing board. Place one chiffon piece onto the parchment. Peel off the backing from both sides of the sandwich, and place it down on the chiffon. Put the other piece of chiffon on top of the sandwich. Then put a piece of baking parchment on top of that. With the iron set at the highest setting, press one section at a time until your sandwich is ironed to itself.

Topstitch the silk chiffon sandwich with variegated rayon thread in a random fashion. Then carefully burn it with a hot air gun. You don't want to set it on fire: You simply want to char the silk, to expose the glitzy threads underneath and create a velvety effect.

Finish the bodice by using free-motion machine embroidery edging along the bottom. Place a piece of water-soluble stabilizer under the silk, then stitch. You'll want to start off with some straight stitches and then lock in your design by crossing over each one several times with some short zigzag stitches.

Place the bodice in room temperature water, and dissolve the stabilizer. Let the bodice air dry. Set it aside for now.

Creating Tyvek Beads

Tyvek is part paper and part fiber, so it doesn't tear easily. Express Mail and FedEx envelopes are made from medium-weight Tyvek; clothing and environmental suits, from fabric-weight Tyvek; and housing insulation, from heavy-weight Tyvek. For doll making, medium-weight and fabric-weight Tyvek are best. You'll want to avoid using the heavy-weight Tyvek because it has chemicals in it. (See Resources, page 118.)

Cut some strips of Tyvek, and color both sides with acrylic or fabric paints, crayons, or markers. Let dry.

Cut these in smaller pieces of varying shapes, about 1" x 3" (2.5 x 7.5 cm). Wrap about three of the shapes and colors onto a wooden skewer, securing them with metallic thread. Using the lower setting on a hot air gun, melt the Tyvek together, to create a beautiful bead.

Using the lower setting on a hot air gun, melt the Tyvek together, to create a beautiful bead.

Carefully remove the bead from the skewer and make as many as you need to embellish the doll.

Take some Tyvek beads, and string them on some yarn. Tie several overhand knots in the ends to keep the beads from falling off the yarn. Topstitch these to the bottom of the bodice.

Applying Covered Washers

Hardware stores are a great place to find unique doll-making supplies. Washers are a good example. Eileen Lyons was the source on this one; see her doll in the Gallery, page 60.

First you'll need to cover the washers, using some yarn that matches the doll's outfit and a tapestry needle. The stitch used to cover the washers is called "button hole." If you don't know it, it's extremely easy to learn.

Leave the yarn on the spool. Thread the cut end through the tapestry needle, leaving about 1 yard (91.5 cm) to work with. (This means you'll pull 1 yard (91.5 cm) of the yarn off the spool.) Take the needle through the inside of the washer, and come up and under the loose end. Go back through the center of the washer and up under the loose end. Continue doing this until you've gone completely around the washer. Cut the yarn from the spool, and tie at the washer and again at the top. Topstitch this onto the bodice. Make as many covered washers as you want, and attach them to the bodice or leave some for other parts of the clothing.

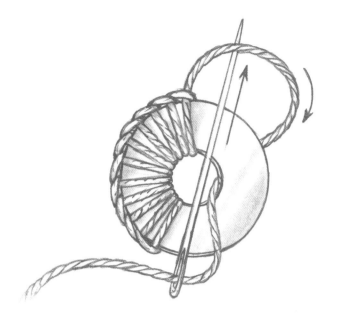

Cover the washers using the "button hole stitch."

Completing the Bodice

Once the bodice is embellished to your liking, pin it to the doll's body. Overlap the raw ends at her back, and ladder stitch or whipstitch it closed. Tuck in here and there using a needle and thread. Because the bodice is so embellished, the threads won't show.

Making Sleeves

The sample doll's sleeves were knitted and then finished with a crocheted edging. An alternative is to create sleeves from fabric. To recreate the knitted look, follow the steps below:

1. Using size 4 knitting needles, cast on 33.

2. Knit 29 rows.

3. Row 30: Knit 3, knit 2 together, repeat 5 times, knit 3.

4. Row 31: Knit.

5. Row 32: Knit 3, knit 2 together, repeat 4 times, knit 2.

6. Row 33: Knit.

7. Bind off, and leave a 7" (18 cm) tail.

8. Thread the yarn through a tapestry needle, and sew the sides together to form the sleeve.

9. To create the edging, anchor glitzy yarn at the bottom of the sleeve with a size D crochet hook. Chain 3. In the starting stitch of the knitted edge, double crochet 2 times. In the next stitch of the sleeve edge, double crochet 3 times. Continue around the edge of the sleeve with 3 double crochets in each stitch, to create a lacy effect.

10. Slip the sleeves onto the doll, and tack them to the shoulders using a needle and thread.

Creating Tyvek Clusters

Paint some light-weight or fabric-weight Tyvek using the colors of your choice. Let dry. Cut out various shapes. Hold these down on tile or aluminum foil with a wooden skewer, and apply heat with a hot air gun. The shapes will curl up on themselves. As you heat them, you can move them around with the skewer. Set them aside to cool.

Apply the clusters to the doll's sleeves to add interest. You might also place some on her head and add some Tyvek beads to the clusters as a further embellishment. The Tyvek remains soft, so you can sew the clusters using a regular needle and thread.

Creating Shoes

Trace the shoe pattern onto a piece of water-soluble stabilizer. Trace two for each foot for a total of four. Then trace two soles.

Place metallic thread in your bobbin and variegated rayon thread in your machine. Lower your feed dog, and use a darning foot or free-motion foot in your machine. (Keep in mind that when doing free-motion machine embroidery, you don't want the foot to touch the plate of the machine.)

Sew the outline of the shoes, then sew in a grid. The grid lays down a base that will prevent your decorative or free motion stitches from falling apart after the stabilizer is removed. To create a grid, stitch horizontally, back and forth across the piece from one side of the outline to the other. Then, stitch vertically, up and down the piece, to create perpendicular lines across the rows, thereby creating a grid. Dissolve the stabilizer.

When the pieces are dry, hand sew the top of the shoes together, and place them on the doll's feet. Hand sew the soles to the bottoms of the shoes while they're on her feet. Catch her feet occasionally to secure them.

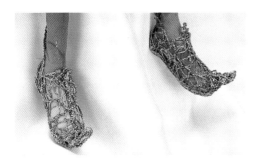

Giving the Doll Wings

Trace two wings onto the water-soluble stabilizer. Sew along the outline, then do the grid work. After the grid work is done, set your machine to the zigzag stitch, and fill in the centers of the design.

When the wings are to your liking, zigzag over some beading wire to stabilize them. Then put them in water to dissolve away the stabilizer. When the wings are dry, tack them to the doll's back.

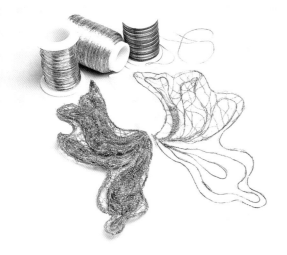

Adding Cuffs to the Wrists

Draw a design on the stabilizer and free-motion machine embroider. When you're done, put the cuffs in water to dissolve away the stabilizer. When they're dry, tack them onto the doll's arms.

Attaching Hair to the Head

On the sample doll, mohair was used. Cluster the mohair, and sew it along the hairline. Fluff it up and arrange it using a felting needle or a needle and thread. Sew some Tyvek clusters toward the front of her hairline. Then add some Tyvek beads.

What a beauty!

Take Me to the Tropics

ARTIST: Barbara Carleton Evans   (Pattern: Doll #1)

"Take me to the Tropics (I've had enough of Winter) began in my fabric stash. I wanted something attention-grabbing, so I chose purple suede and used it to sew the doll on the machine. To transfer the pattern to suede, I cut pattern pieces out of freezer paper, ironed them onto the wrong side of the suede, placed that suede piece on top of another suede piece (right sides together), and machine stitched around the pattern. After stitching, I trimmed each piece and peeled off the freezer paper pattern. (Thanks to Louise Mendenhall for that nifty trick.) Because of the stiffness of the suede, I didn't thread-wrap the elbow joints. I attached the arms just like the legs. Before assembling the body, I lightly brushed the surfaces with stenciling paint.

I used natural fiber yarns for hair, hand-dyed by Kate Stephenson. The hair ornaments began with a little green parrot. After attaching him, I added bits and pieces. The tube bead is made from a rolled up postage stamp (first class, of course).

The doll's garment is a loosely crocheted neck scarf. The purple metallic yarn looks good with the doll's body color. The combination of the body color, garment color, and the parrot gave the doll a neat tropical theme.

Finally, I added postage stamps, costume jewelry pins, green glass leaf-shaped beads, vintage fabric flowers, and buttons to embellish the body, and I cut the guitar player from the back of an old playing card."

Arianne

ARTIST: Di McDonald   (Pattern: Doll #1)

"What fun this doll was to make! At first I planned to straighten her legs and wire her body so she could stand and show off her clothes. After thinking about it a little I decided to go with the pattern and change the joints and hands. I especially loved her feet: She looked so graceful, just like a ballerina. Bright colors are my favorites, so I chose a very fine bright orange silk, which was shot with hot pink. To go with this I found some hot pink chiffon, Tyvek, assorted threads, yarns, beads, and sequins.

Wrapping is one of the techniques I am playing with right now, so after I made the body, I ripped strips of silk and wrapped the arms, legs, and body. I left her belly button showing to give her a trendier look. Over this I used metallic threads. I also painted a sheet of Tyvek with Lumiere paints, ripped more strips of the silk, and glued them to the Tyvek. I then cut the Tyvek into strips and rolled them into beads. I used embossing powder and a heat gun to give the beads unusual shapes. These beads made great edging for the off-center neckline and the skirt. The rest of the beads I threaded onto copper wire and made a belt.

I painted the ballet slippers with Lumiere paints, and I used various sequins and beads to decorate them. I added multiple gathered skirts using the silk, chiffon, and white tulle. I scrunched, sequined, and beaded the sleeves, and gathered and flounced the silk at her wrists.

Black maribu seemed appropriate for her hair, and to top it off I made a turban for her head. Lots of bright colors brought this doll's pretty face to life!"

Gussie of Somerset

ARTIST: Eileen Lyons (Pattern: Doll #2)

"Using a new dye/fabric paint I colored Tyvek, interfacing, seam binding, cheesecloth, crochet thread, fabric. When everything was colored, I started to play. I used the cheesecloth and the Tyvek to create her blouse. Then I cut the inter-facing and some fabric into triangle shapes, threw them onto a piece of fabric, and started to free-motion machine embroider them. The doll now had her skirt.

For one sleeve, I dyed a piece of lightweight fabric. Then I pulled out the crochet hook and some funky yarns and started to do some free-form crocheting. She ended up with a funky sleeve and hat. For her hair I used some eyelash yarn. Then I crocheted her shoes.

To embellish her, I stitched the plastic rings that you use as markers when you knit from her hat. Finally, I added beaded flowers and leaves on her shoes and some beads and threads around her neckline.

Because I used a lot of yarn and thread, I wanted to name the doll after my aunt in England who was a wonderful yarn artist. Her full name is Augusta of Midsummer-Norton, Somerset NR Bath. I shortened it to Gussie of Somerset."

Auriela, the Sea Bride

ARTIST: Ann Maullin (Pattern: Mixed)

"This doll was inspired by the wonderful blue and green colors in a pack of merino wool I purchased. I gathered some matching silk, mohair, organza, tulle, and some great yarns and sketched some sea figures sitting on shells, using lots of wavy motifs.

I made a piece of felt and some free-form crochet and knitted motifs using my collection. I thought the doll's wonderful body shape, the felt, and the motifs would be lost if she were sitting, so I made her a standing doll, with an internal stand. I also wanted her to portray movement, so I bent her at the waist and posed her arms and legs.

I used the patterns for upper and lower arms and upper and lower legs from Doll #3. I added the foot from Doll #1 and the body and head from Doll #2. I also sewed a dart into the body so she would bend.

Because felt stretches slightly in length when stuffed, I decided to omit the arm and leg joints and sew the upper arm and leg to the lower arm and leg. I lightly needle-sculpted a knee on the leg.

I dyed the pantyhose, organza, and bridal tulle. I cut the organza and tulle into a triangle and edged with a 40-lb (18 kg) fishing line, which I attached using the zigzag stitch. Then I slashed the tulle to form two trails and draped them onto the doll."

Tarni, Barrier Reef Princess

ARTIST: Wendy Fenwick   (Pattern: Doll #3)

"For me, Tarni depicts the glorious colors of Australia and the textures of the Great Barrier Reef. Her 'royal robe' uses many techniques, textures, and colors to capture the beautiful coral beds and reef life. Her dress is made from crinkled silky fabric, to look like water glistening in the sun and pooling around her feet.

I used various fabrics, yarns, laces, silk ribbons, and embroideries, dying them when necessary to match my color palette. I chose the clear blue silk fabric for the robe, overlaying darker blue lace around the bottom edge for depth. I appliquéd tulle for seaweed. I added knitting and crochet yarns for coral shapes and robe 'fur' edging trim for textural effect.

Before I arranged my design and colors, I made many wide ruffles to give the seaweed a 3-D effect. These strips consisted of dyed silks, metallics, and organzas, cut on the bias, doubled in half, with fishing line inside the fold and fancy threads satin stitched along the fold edge of ruffle. I sewed the raw edges with a gathering stitch pulled tight to flute the fabrics. I tucked in knitted and crocheted fancy yarns for coral.

I appliquéd all embroidered designs with transparent thread and completed Tarni's ensemble with little sandals, made from felted merino fleece and silk fibers, dyed to match water colors, and beaded.

Finally, I adorned her starfish crown and necklace with crystals and seed beads and her sea horse with topaz chips and crystal eyes."

Huldra, Troll Maiden

ARTIST: Ute Vasina (Pattern: Doll #3)

"Considering that I'm used to making all my dolls from doe suede and with troll-like features, this doll posed an interesting challenge. The first thing I did was make her nose larger. (I have this thing about noses.) The next step was the torso. I really liked the womanly figure! She didn't resemble any of my troll figures. I decided she would be 'Huldra,' appearing like a fair maiden—a beautiful seductress from the outside, but very much a troll from within. After all, some female trolls will do that to find or catch a husband.

With this is mind, she took on a great form, right down to her toes. I almost hated putting clothes on her. With her strong personality, I had a sense right from the start what she wanted, so her clothes are very simple, her sweater hand-knit, and her hair made from mohair.

Finally, I love to recycle old or used things. For some dolls, I'll use a piece of clothing. For others, I'll add something old, such as an old skeleton key, a piece of jewelry, or another great find. In Huldra's hand I've placed a very special key.

This doll has a real peaceful elegance about her. Maybe it's the beauty shining from within."

Beading

Doing peyote beadwork and bead embroidery

4

Beading can add a wonderful level of embellishment to your doll creations. In addition to using Tyvek beads, which were featured in the last chapter, you'll learn to make wrapped beads and peyote flowers and do other types of free-form beading. Beads can be used for everything from simple, delicate adornments to more elaborate ones like the obsessive beauty of a beaded mermaid's tail, as seen on page 79.

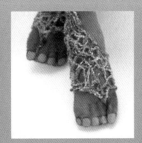

Advanced Doll

So far you've learned how to make a beginning doll and an intermediate doll. In this chapter, you'll learn to make a more advanced doll, Dahlianna (Doll #3). What makes her more advanced? She has a chin gusset, fully articulated fingers, a more complicated bust overlay, and different joints.

After you've made this doll, you can dye her, as discussed in Chapter 2 on page 30, or you can use other fabrics to give the look of flesh. You may even want to make her from patterned fabric for a really unique look. Once the body is fully constructed, you'll learn to create beautiful bead-work to adorn her. The clothing on this doll is made primarily with dyed cheesecloth, to allow her ornamented body to show through.

Supplies

¹/₄ yard (23 cm) pima cotton

matching thread

scissors

hemostats

stuffing

stuffing fork

6 pipe cleaners

hand-sewing needles

3" (7.5 cm) needle and strong thread for attaching the arms and legs

Zig or Micron pens: black, brown, red

16 small buttons or accent beads for joints

cotton or wool batting for joints

Jacquard's Dye-NA-Flow paints in colors of your choice (The sample doll was dyed using magenta, chartreuse, violet, and green. Also, the flesh formula from the last two chapters was used for her face, neck, and part of her chest.)

cheesecloth (the kind found at grocery stores)

5 different decorative yarns for making fabric beads

size 10 or 12 beading needle

Nymo beading thread

beeswax

7 colors size 11 seed beads

accent beads for centers of flowers

small sheet of medium-weight Tyvek

mechanical pencil and eraser

colored pencils

Pentel gel pens: white, black, purple

2 colors size 6 seed beads

floral beads

tapestry needle

heat gun

metallic threads

variegated rayon thread

wooden skewer

silk ribbon dyed to match your color scheme

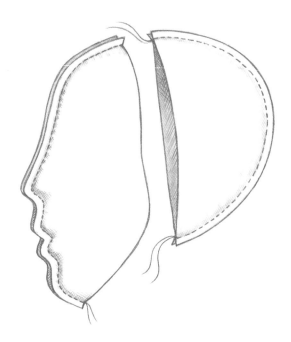

[step 3]
The Face and Head Back have tracing and sewing
seams. Sew seam #1 on the Face and
seam #2 on the Head Back.

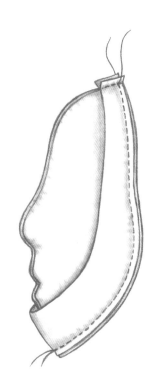

[step 4]
There will be a seam allowance at the
top of the Face Gusset. Sew across this now.

Making the Body

1. Arrange and trace all patterns for Doll #3 onto the wrong side of the body fabric. (See Chapter 1, page 14.) Then double the fabric, right sides together, and pin in several places. Trace the Body Front onto a single layer of fabric. (This piece won't be doubled.)

2. When tracing the head pieces, notice that the Face Gusset has a grain line. Fold your fabric here so you have some stretch in the cheek area when you fill it with stuffing.

3. Begin by sewing the headpieces. The Face and Head Back have tracing and sewing seams. Sew seam #1 on the Face and seam #2 on the Head Back.

4. Cut out all three pieces for the head. Pin the Face Gusset, matching from the center of the chin at seam #3 on the Face to seam #3 on the Gusset, right sides together. Sew from the chin up to the top on one side, then from the chin to the top on the other side. There will be a seam allowance at the top of the Face Gusset. Sew across this now.

5. Pin the Head Back to the Face Gusset at seam #4, right sides together. Sew from top down to the X. Do the same on the other side. Keep in mind that you'll want to back-stitch when you get to the X so the seam stays together when you fill the head with stuffing.

6. Clip curves, and turn right side out. Fill firmly with stuffing, then set aside.

7. Sew seam #5 on the Body Back, leaving it open where marked. Cut out both body pieces. Sew in darts on both the Body Back and the Body Front.

8. Pin the Body Back to the Body Front, right sides together, and sew from the opening at the neck around to the other side of the opening at the neck. Be sure to backstitch the neck area. Turn the body right side out, and fill with stuffing.

9. Cut out the Bust pieces. Fold each Bust at the dart, right sides together, and sew along the dashed lines. Turn right side out, and place a small amount of stuffing inside the bust "pocket."

10. Pin each Bust piece to the chest of the Body Front. Turning under just $1/8$" (0.3 cm), start at the center and hand sew the Bust piece to the chest wall, using a ladder stitch. From the center, go up across the collarbone, down a bit by the "under arm," then leave it open here. Finish hand sewing under the Bust, then fill the rest of it with stuffing, and close up the opening.

11. After you attach each Bust piece, create the collarbone. Using a needle and thread, start at the center, hiding the knot under the breast. Come out about $1/4$" (0.6 cm) from center top of the Bust. Take about a $1/4$" (0.6 cm) length stitch across, heading toward the shoulder with the needle going into the Bust and up to the top where you attached it to the chest wall. Hide the stitch at the top, and go back down to $1/4$" (0.6 cm) below this seam, next to the stitch you made above. Go across toward the shoulder as before and then back inside the Bust piece up to the top. Keep doing this up and down stitch until you come to the end of the Bust at the shoulder. Anchor the thread, and cut. What you've done is sculpt the collarbone. As you do the up and down stitches, pull a bit to define the "bone." Do the same to the other Bust.

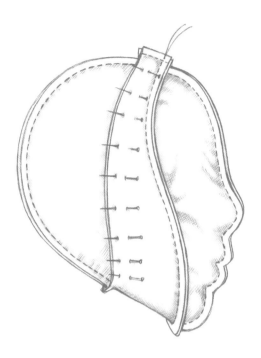

[step 5]
Pin the Head Back to the Face Gusset at seam #4, right sides together.

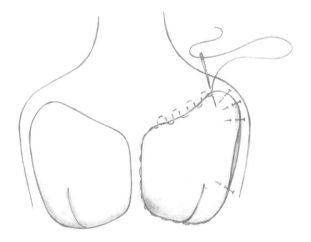

[step 10]
Turning under just $1/8$" (0.3 cm), start at the center and hand sew the Bust piece to the chest wall, using a ladder stitch.

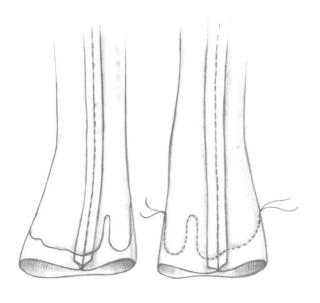

[step 13]
Draw in a big toe and then the other
toes together. Make sure you have both
a right and a left foot.

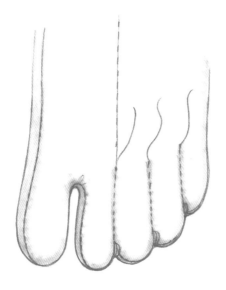

[step 14]
Sculpt the other toes using
a needle and thread.

12. The upper legs are extremely easy. Sew all the way around both Upper Legs. Cut them out, and cut a slit on one side of each leg. Turn through this slit, and fill with stuffing. Close up the slit using a needle and strong thread.

13. To make the lower legs, sew from the opening at the toes around and down to the opening at the toes on the other side, leaving open where marked toward the top of the leg. Cut out the Lower Legs, then draw in the toes before turning. Note that this doll has a separate big toe. Fold the feet so the seams match at the toes. Draw in a big toe and then the other toes together. Make sure you have both a right and a left foot.

14. Next, follow your drawing and stitch the toes. Clip around the curves and in between the big toe. Turn the leg right side out through the opening at the top of the leg. Fill with stuffing, making sure to fill out the big toes. Sculpt the other toes using a needle and thread. First, draw with a pencil where you want the toes to be. Attach thread to the bottom of the foot (her sandals will cover it), and come out at the bottom of the toe, in between two toes. Sew a running stitch from top to bottom, back up to top, and down through fabric to bottom. When you come to about $1/8$" (0.3 cm) from the end of the toe, wrap the thread over the top of the toe, and go into the fabric. Do this with each toe.

Finish by drawing in toenails with the brown Zig pen, and paint her toenails with paint or fingernail polish.

15. Trace four joints onto the wrong side of your fabric. Layer this with batting at the bottom and the fabric on top. The drawing is face up. Sew all the way around. Cut out the joints, and cut a slit in the drawing side on one layer only. Turn through this slit, and close up opening using a needle and thread.

16. Attach the joints to the legs with accent beads or small buttons. These joints show, so use nice beads or buttons.

17. Attach the legs to the body where marked.

18. Sew around the Upper Arm, leaving it open where marked. Cut it out, and turn through this opening. Fill with stuffing, and close the opening.

19. Sew the Lower Arm from the opening at the wrist around to the other side of the wrist opening. Turn, and fill to $\frac{1}{2}$" (1.3 cm) above opening.

20. With a shorter stitch length on your machine, sew the Hands from the opening at the wrist around the fingers to the opening at the wrist on the other side. Follow the instructions in Chapter 3, page 47, for sewing fingers. Cut out the Hands, and finish as described in Chapter 1, pages 15 and 16, for both turning and wiring them.

21. After the Hands are done, insert them into the arms and ladder stitch at the wrists, leaving a small place open to finish filling up wrists with stuffing. Close up this opening.

22. Trace four joints as you did with the legs, and sew. Turn, close up the openings, and attach to Upper Arm and Lower Arm as you did with the legs.

23. Attach the arms to the shoulders, using the long needle and strong thread. Run the needle back and forth through the body as you did with the legs.

24. Draw the features on her face following the guidelines in Chapter 1, pages 17 to 19, then sculpt as described in Chapter 3, page 49.

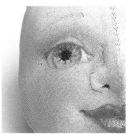

25. Now dye the face and body and color the face as described in Chapter 3, page 50. You can also refer to Chapter 5 for more ideas on faces.

26. While you have the dyes out, dye the cheesecloth. Dry everything thoroughly, then heat set everything either by placing the doll and the cheesecloth on a sweater rack in your clothes dryer or by ironing.

Embellishing with Beads

The techniques featured here include making a wrapped bead, making a simple peyote-beaded flower, and doing free-form peyote beadwork, which helps to create an undulating look by using different sizes of beads.

Beading is a fun way to add texture and interest to your doll. This art form has been around forever, and many terrific books are available on the history of beading.

1. To make a wrapped bead, cut each of the five different yarns into 3-yard (2.7 m) lengths. Tie one of the ends together. Move down about ¹/₂" (1.3 cm), and take 1 yarn and wrap it around the others until you get a shape that looks somewhat like a bead.

2. To secure this "bundle," thread your beading needle with 1¹/₂ yards (1.5 m) of beading thread. Put a knot in the end, and anchor this thread under the yarn bead. String on enough beads to go over the top of the yarn bead. Run the needle under the bead, and string up more beads to do the same. Keep adding rows of beads to add interest to your yarn bead.

3. Wrap another yarn around the rest of the yarns underneath your bead for about ¹/₂" (1.3 cm). Wrap another yarn bead. This time use one of your other yarns, and secure the yarn bead by coming out under the bead and then going over it, down under the bead and up again.

4. Continue wrapping and creating beads, sometimes using seed beads and other times using yarns to secure the yarn beads. You can do some latticework with yarns, too, or you can do needle lacing or crochet.

5. When you've gone the full length of the yarns, tie an overhand knot to secure everything. Set this aside for now. You can use this for her headband, which you'll complete toward the end of the project. (If you did it now it would be in the way.)

6. For the peyote-beaded flowers, you'll need the seed beads, beading needle, and nymo thread. Even if you haven't done peyote beadwork before, these flowers are simple to make, and the leaves are made using the same steps.

7. Start by cutting a 1-yard (91.5 cm) length of the nymo thread. Thread the beading needle with this. (To make threading easier, lick the eye of the needle, then thread it.) Because no stress will be placed on these petals, single thread is sufficient. Also, it helps to wax the thread with beading or beeswax to prevent the thread from knotting up. Pick up 12 of the size 11 seed beads, all in a single color. Run them to the bottom of the thread, leaving a 3" (7.5 cm) tail.

8. Skip beads 12, 11, and 10, and go through bead 9. (You're heading back toward the tail.) Go only through one bead, bead 9. Add a bead, skip bead 8, and go through bead 7. Add another bead, skip bead 6, and go through bead 5. Add a bead, skip bead 4, and go through bead 3. Add a bead, skip bead 2, and go through bead 1. Now you've done peyote beadwork and learned the peyote chant: Add, skip, go through! Fun, right?

9. At the bottom where your tail is, tie the two threads together in an overhand knot, twice. Head back the other way by adding a bead, and go through the "up" bead (the last bead you put on in the previous row). You've still skipped a bead, the "down" bead, or bead 1 where it all began. Continue on by adding another bead, skip the "down" bead, and go through the "up" bead. Add another bead, skip the "down" bead, and go through the "up" bead. Stop. You want to see two more "up" beads. Next, add two beads (you'll do this only once on each side), go back down toward the tail, and go through the "up" bead. Add a bead, skip the "down" bead, and go through the "up" bead and on down through the last two beads. This technique is different, but the beadwork here is the end of one petal, and it needs to be thinner than the midpart of the petal.

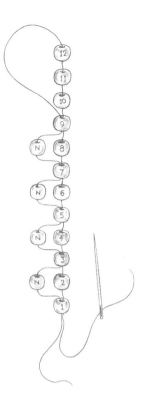

[step 8]
Add interest with peyote beadwork.

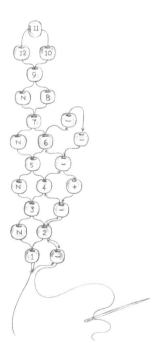

[step 9]
At the bottom where your tail is, tie the two threads together in an overhand knot, twice.

10. Your needle is at the bottom of the work. Take the needle over to the next bead at the bottom, and go up through two beads. Add a bead, skip the "down" bead, and go through the "up" bead. Add a bead, skip the "down" bead, and go through the "up" bead. Stop. You're at the same point as you were on the other side. Add two beads, go down toward the bottom and through the "up" bead, add a bead, and go through the next three beads. You're at the bottom again. You now have one complete petal.

11. Next to this petal, create two more petals using the same color beads. The bottom part of your flower—the three petals that are connected—is done. Secure the petals by weaving your thread in and out of the beads at the bottom of each petal.

12. Change colors, and create three more petals. These will remain on the top of the three lower petals. Secure them using a needle and thread.

13. At the center of each flower, add an accent bead. This can be a beautiful Austrian crystal or any another type of bead. Make as many flowers as you want. Change your colors around. The sample doll has 15 flowers.

14. Use the same pattern for the leaves, but do only half of the petal. So instead of having two sides with points, you'll have only one side. This creates the look of a leaf.

15. Start tacking the petals to her arms, then string some green beads along her arm to create the look of vines. Add some leaves to the vines, and continue tacking on the flowers.

16. Before tacking flowers to her bodice, you'll want to add some clothing. Her bodice is done the same way as for Doll #1 in Chapter 2. Loop two strips of cheesecloth around each other, then tie it at the back. Sew it in place using a needle and thread. Cut some smaller strips of cheesecloth, and arrange them at her shoulders.

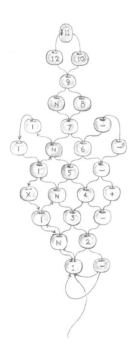

[step 10]
Your needle is at the bottom of the work. Take the needle over to the next bead at the bottom, and go up through two beads.

74

17. Once her bodice is in place, you can tack on some flowers. Leave room for some free-form peyote beadwork.

18. To begin, thread a beading needle with 2 yards (1.8 m) of beading thread. As with the flowers, you don't need to double it. You'll need two colors of size 11 seed beads and one color of size 6 seed beads. Pick up two of each of these beads on your needle and thread. Six total. Add a bead, skip bead 6 and go through bead 5, add a bead, skip bead 4 and go through bead 3. Add a bead, skip bead 2 and go through bead 1. When adding the beads, change sizes. Keep doing these rows until you have the length you want. Add some accent beads every once-in-awhile to give a more undulating effect.

19. Once you have the look you want, tack it to her bodice. Add more flowers and leaves.

20. Tack a flower on each of the arms where you attached them to the body. These add a nice touch to cover those stitches.

21. To make her skirt, use a strip of the cheese-cloth, and tack it to her body just below her waist. Cover that with a narrow strip of cheesecloth that has been dyed a different color, then cover that with some fancy yarns. Sew on some accent beads here and there along the top edge of the skirt.

22. Make some Tyvek beads. (See Chapter 3, page 54.) Add them to some of the yarns, and tack along her waist. Allow the Tyvek beads to dangle from the waist. Slip some larger beads on the bottom of the cheese-cloth strip that's at her waist.

23. Her headpiece is another strip of cheesecloth that's wrapped around her head and tied at the top. Wrap the yarn beads you created around this, as shown on the sample doll, and secure in place using needle and thread. Add some more strips of cheesecloth at the top and a beaded flower to one side.

24. Her shoes are done using free-motion machine embroidery on water-soluble stabi-lizer. Trace the bottoms of her left foot and her right foot onto the stabilizer. Next lay the stabilizer on top of her feet, and trace the design you want. Sew in your design, and dissolve the stabilizer. (See Chapter 3, pages 56 and 57, for more on this process.)

25. Attach her sandals to her feet using a needle and thread. Secure a few beads here and there, then add some silk ribbons and some beaded flowers to the top.

Wishing Fairie

ARTIST: Annie Hesse   (Pattern: Doll #1)

"When I teach a class, I always tell my students to find the easiest methods to reach the desired end. So, I followed my own advice and chose the beginner pattern, enlarging it to 110%. I used the advanced hand, though, because I like articulated fingers.

The body shape was so nice that I decided to create my own fabric. I used white 100% cotton fabric and painted it with Jacquard's Lumiere paints—green, gold, and copper. I then stamped images on the dry surface and ironed the fabric to set the colors. I traced the pattern pieces onto the wrong side of my painted fabric, then sewed, cut out, turned, and filled the body with stuffing.

For the beading, I used bead embroidery techniques. I traced my design onto the face and then started laying down my beads and tacking them in place to the fabric. When the face was complete, I attached it to the neck of the doll.

I created the hair with yarns, the skirt and sleeves with tulle, and the necklace with strands of beads. As a final touch, I painted a papier-mâché star and placed it on a stick, which I also painted."

Goddess of Fauna

ARTIST: Dorice Larkin   (Pattern: Doll #1)

"First I sewed and stuffed the body, dyed it with
earth-tone colors, and heat set the colors in the
clothes dryer. Then I created her embellishments.

I used some raffia to create a grass skirt. Over
this I placed a beaded belt. To create the
belt, I beaded over a piece of felt, using
random bead embroidery. (This was both
simple and quick to do: You lay down a
row of beads and then go through every
third bead into the felt to hold the design
in place.)

The beads at her neck were also easy to
make. First I strung enough beads to make
the neck piece the length I wanted. Then
starting from the end, I added nine more beads
in contrasting color. I counted over five beads from
my original beads and entered the fifth bead. I continued this to the end of the strand. Then I turned
my needle and went back toward the opposite
end, going through five beads and adding an
accent bead. I placed this bead at the opposite
side of the strand from the picot I created above.
I went through five
more beads and added
an accent bead, contin-
uing this to the end."

Beaded Garden

ARTIST: Kathy Gaines (Pattern: Doll#3)

"I used Pimatex fabric for the doll's body and woven silk for her clothes, flowers, and leaves. I also dyed the entire doll using Jacquard's Dye-NA-Flow paints. First I slightly diluted the dyes with water (sulfur green, emerald green, sun yellow, violet, and hot fuchsia), then I applied the dye to fabric that had been moistened with water, to achieve a soft effect.

The lined and seamless skirt is circular with a scalloped edge. The waistline is set off-center. I finished the edges of the skirt and sleeves with a beaded scallop and covered the sleeves with vertical netting. For the necklace, I used circular netting.

I made the collar using free-form peyote beadwork. As I beaded the rows, decreases at the neck edge shaped the collar to fit the neckline. I then layered the collar with flower beads and fluffies. I came out of a bead, added a loop of three to five beads, and backstitched through the other side.

To make the sandals, I traced around the doll's feet onto a piece of cardboard, and then I glued fabric to the cardboard, tucking under the raw edges. I cut the soles and heels from leather and glued them to the fabric base. Finally, I created a peyote-beaded strip to fit on the top of the doll's foot and embellished it with beaded flowers, flower beads, and leaves."

Oasis

ARTIST: Michelle Meinhold   (Pattern: Doll#2)

"Doll making is my love, but beading is my passion. Oasis, my mermaid, merges these obsessions. With the help of my dear friend Kandra Norsigian, my seed bead colors were chosen. Once the bead colors were in place, I found the fin fabric and fibers for her hair and soon everything went together.

The scales are done in Japanese 14 seed beads. I used a flat peyote stitch to make each row of scales. The scale design is done in a Bargello pattern, with the shading going from a dark purple to a pale yellow green. Once a row was completed, I stitched it to the already stuffed fabric body. I wired her fin using an 18-gauge wire, and then I embellished her fin with Swarovski crystals and amethyst beads along with Japanese 11 seed beads. To finish off her waistline, I did a double-twist stitch with 11s, fresh water pearls, and vintage Swarovski crystals.

I also used 14s and flat peyote to make the seashells that cover her bust. To complete the doll, I made beaded beads with 3-mm Swarovski crystals and 14s for her elbow joints. For her hair I used Prism fibers."

Anii

ARTIST: Lynne Butcher   (Pattern: Doll#3)

"For this doll I used the advanced pattern and stretched a lycra skin over the cotton body. I then added stuffing between the layers to create contours and fullness where needed. Instead of using the joints, I butted the body pieces together, to give a smooth look to the body. Once the body was finished, I decided not to cover her with bulky clothing. I found an old delicate piece of lace in a secondhand store. I liked the lace's earthy color, and when I cut it into smaller pieces and arranged it on the body, it immediately looked like lichen.

After attaching her 'clothing,' I randomly sewed tiny beads to her body. Ruth Stonely, a well-known Australian quilter and embroiderer, told me that when randomly beading, the aim is to make the beads look as though they've been tipped over the fabric and stitched on just where they lay. I tried to achieve this.

After I made the head, I stretched lycra over the face and needle-sculpted it, adding pieces of stuffing between the layers to form cheekbones, eyeballs, and a stronger nose. I used Prismacolor pencils and a fine Permawriter pen to outline and define features. I embroidered on the eyelashes and used strands of yarns for the hair and threads with beads to tie it all together."

Anapelli

ARTIST: Kandy Scott (Pattern: Doll#3)

"Anapelli has a wonderfully curvy body, so I didn't want to cover it up with too many clothes. She's wearing a modest beaded bodice with a shawl collar that meets in the back with a beaded tassel.

The beads are an assortment of organic-looking beads from thrift store necklaces and Tyvek beads. I made the medallion on her skirt from painted pieces of Tyvek. First I cut odd-shaped pieces of the material in various colors, then I heated it from the unpainted side. I stacked various pieces until I came up with a pleasing configuration. Then I glued them together.

For her skirt, I fused my main fabric together so that no wrong side showed. Then I cut long curvy pieces, embellished them with couched yarn, and sewed them all to a band that fits around her hips. I also strung wooden beads, Tyvek beads, and seed beads on pieces of yarn and sewed them to the waistband. Her tree was made of coat hangers and attached to a doll stand base, which was then wrapped with torn strips of fabric and yarn. Two branches were bent in the back to go under her armpits so she could relax and feel secure while waiting for the moon to rise and the stars to splash across the sky."

Collage

Working with fabric, beading, and photo transfer

Collage is an art form that doll makers have used for a long time. It involves combining various types of materials to create a unique piece of art. Generally, when you think of collage, paper and decoupage come to mind. But in this doll project, you'll use fabric, yarn, beads, paints, and stamps as well. You can draw inspiration from the gallery sections in this chapter and in others throughout the book, or you can simply rely on your own creativity. It's up to you.

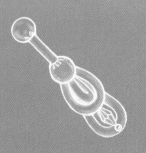

The Collage Doll

This sample doll, named Down Memory Lane, uses several forms of collage. To begin with, she combines all three patterns—her body is from Doll #2, her arms are from Doll #1, and her head, hands, and legs are from Doll #3.

Before the body is made, a decorative fabric is created using collage techniques. Then the main body parts are cut from this fabric. Her face, hands, feet, and upper chest are all done in flesh tones. More detailed face instructions are discussed in this chapter along with using a different type of stamping material. Remember: It's good to experiment with different mediums. Also, don't let a label throw you off—if you like a product, go ahead and try it on fabric.

Incorporating collaged materials into your dolls will open up a whole world of design possibilities. You can use collage to explore all types of textures and themes, transforming your doll into a true work of art.

Supplies

photos

photo-ready fabric

scissors

rayon and metallic threads for machine embroidery

fabrics for making collage body (batiks, prints, solids, and so on)

fat quarter-pima cotton for face, bust, hands, and feet

threads to match

stuffing

stuffing and turning tools

yarns (including glitzy ones)

fine netting

pins

face supplies

Tsukineko's All Purpose Inks: sand, white, autumn leaf, cherry pink, and other colors of your choice

paint brushes and containers for mixing paints

paper towels

Tsukineko's Fantastix (looks like empty markers)

Brilliance stamp pads

rubber stamps

hand-sewing needles

strong thread for sculpting

beads: beading needles and thread

accent beads

old lace or trims

crochet hook

tulle

Lucet

[step 1]
In the sample doll, squares and stars were
cut from various fabrics, in various sizes.

[step 2]
Peel off the paper backing, and cut
out the photos you want to use.

Making the Body

1. Before cutting out the body parts, create a collage of fabrics and designs to form the main part of the doll's body. In the sample doll, squares and stars were cut from various fabrics, in various sizes. The smaller square had a "window" cut in the center.

2. Using the photo-ready fabric, have some pictures copied onto the fabric. If you have a copy machine at home, you can do this easily yourself. If you don't, you can go to your local copy center. Peel off the paper backing, and cut out the photos you want to use.

3. Place the shapes and photos on the main fabric, and free-motion machine embroider them in place.

4. Using Body for Doll #2, page 110, make your templates. On the Center Body Front, draw across the bust and add a seam allowance on each side, above and below the drawn line. Make a template from this.

5. On the wrong side of the collaged fabric created, lay out the body pieces, except for the top of the Center Body Front, which you'll do in flesh or white fabric. Following the construction of this pattern in Chapter 3, page 44, put the body together. The only difference will be the Center Body Front, which you'll sew together at the center bust then match to the Side Body Front as in Chapter 3.

6. The legs (but not the feet) are from Doll #3 page 113. Simply draw a line at the ankle, adding seam allowance. Then trace the feet from Doll #2, page 109, adding a seam allowance at the ankle.

7. Then trace the Upper Leg and Lower Leg (minus the feet) onto the wrong side of one fabric. (The sample doll uses striped fabric for one side and the created fabric from step 1 for the other side.) Sew as instructed in Chapter 4, page 70.

8. Sew the feet as instructed in Chapter 3, page 45.

9. Fill everything with stuffing. Insert the feet into the Lower Leg, and ladder stitch at ankle.

10. One side of the arms uses a pretty fabric that's created in a unique way: On the right side of one fabric, lay down all kinds of yarns and metallic threads. On top of this, place some fine netting. Pin in several places.

11. Free-motion machine embroider this together to make a beautiful piece of fabric.

12. The sample doll uses the arms from Doll #1, page 107, and the hands from Doll #3, page 112. Trace two arms onto the wrong side of your fabric of choice, then use the above fabric as the other side, and pin the right sides of both fabrics together. Sew, cut out, turn, and fill with stuffing.

13. The hands are done as in Chapter 4, page 71, with the exception that they're separated from the arm. Follow the instructions for turning, wiring, and filling them with stuffing. Insert the hands into the arms at the wrist, and ladder stitch them together.

14. The head is created from Doll #3, page 111, following the instructions in Chapter 4, page 68.

[step 10]
On the right side of the fabric, lay down all kinds of yarns and metallic threads.

Coloring the Face and Chest

1. Draw and sculpt the face, according to the instructions in Chapter 1, pages 17 to 19 and chapter 3, page 49. Then add color either using Tsukineko's All Purpose Inks or dying your doll as you did in the other chapters.

2. For the flesh, mix sand, white, and autumn leaf. Add water, then brush on the entire face and chest.

3. While the color is still wet, pour some left-over flesh color into a container, and add a couple drops of cherry pink for her cheeks. Dip a brush in the ink, and dab it on some paper towels. Now dab it on her cheeks. If it's too bright, use another brush and add more flesh color.

4. Pour some flesh color into another container, and add about 4 drops of sand to this. Add the shading to the side of her face that will be in the shade. Follow the coloring of the face in Chapter 3, page 50. Instead of pencils you'll use ink.

5. After the face is dry, use the Fantastix, and load them with the inks of your choice. Color in the iris by starting with a light color then adding dark to the side of the eye in the shadow.

6. Do the same with the lips.

7. When this is all dry, color in the whites of the eyes with the white ink.

8. After the face is dry, use your pens to add detail.

9. Using the Brilliance stamp pads, stamp her chest and face as you wish. On the sample doll, a Fantastix was dabbed on the Brilliance ink pad and then brushed on her eyelids and eye creases, and stamped images were added for more color.

10. Color or dye her hands and feet. (If you are going to sculpt her toes, do so before coloring.)

[step 9]
On the sample doll, a Fantastix was dabbed on the Brilliance ink pad and then brushed on her eyelids and eye creases, and stamped images were added for more color.

Embellishing the Joints

Using some leftover fabric, beads, and yarns, you can embellish the joints in a truly unique way. You'll want to make at least four of these joints, to go along with the collage theme and to replace the joints from the pattern for Doll #3. You can also make a fifth one, and add it to her belt as the sample doll shows.

1. Cut two 12" x 1" (30.5 x 2.5-cm) strips from three of your fabrics, on the bias.

2. With right sides together, sew these strips, lengthwise, into tubes.

3. Turn using the brass tubes you use to turn fingers or whatever other tool you prefer to use.

4. Decide how you want your colors to go, and cut one strip 1½" (4 cm) long, one strip 3½" (9 cm) long, and the last one 2½" (6.5 cm) long.

5. Cut another piece of fabric (a different color from above) so that it measures 1½" x 1" (4 x 2.5 cm). Finger press one long edge under ⅛" (0.3 cm).

6. Sew the strips together at the top. Fold the short one in half, and position it so that it's facing you. The longer one goes on either side of this, looping it down and up; the medium one, on the outside of the longer one, looping down in front and up.

7. Cover the top of the bundle with the piece of fabric you cut in step 5. Fold under the back, and ladder stitch up the back. Sew along the folded edge, catching the loops as you sew. This secures them so they don't fall out. About ⅛" (0.3 cm) down from the top, sew a running stitch around the top. Leave the needle and thread in for the time being. The strap will be done next, then the dangle will be finished.

8. From one of the tubes, cut a ¾" (2 cm) length. Tuck one end in the top of the bundle, and pull the threads to fit tightly around the strap. Poke the raw edges of the top of the bundle under, and hand stitch the bundle to the strap.

9. The top of the strap is covered with a circle of fabric. Cut out a ¾" (2 cm) circle. Sew a running stitch along the edge, and start to pull. Place the top of the strap inside, and pull circle to fit snugly around the strap. Sew in place.

10. Wrap glitzy yarn around the top of the strap, then run it down to the bundle around the dangles. On the center loop at the bottom, sew a drop or accent bead.

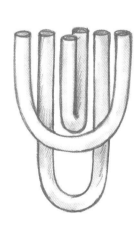

Attaching the Joints and Finishing the Legs

1. Sew one joint at the bottom of her Upper Leg and at the top of her Lower Leg—that is, one on each side of her leg. Do the same on her other leg.

2. Sew her legs to her body, as done in Chapter 4, page 71.

3. Paint some lace to match your color theme. When it's dry, cut two 7" (18 cm) lengths, and hand sew a running stitch along the top edge. Pull to gather, and fit where the feet meet at the ankle. Tack in place.

4. Dye an appliqué motif, and hand sew at ankle of one leg and on the thigh of the other leg.

Finishing the Arms

1. After her hands are dry, color in her fingernails with either the inks or a marker.

2. Using the inks, color a piece of old lace. (Thrift stores are a good place to find old lace if you don't have some handy.)

3. Tack the lace to the arms. Have a bit of it spill over onto the hands.

4. Attach the arms to the body at the shoulders with a needle and strong thread, as done in Chapter 2, page 25.

5. To cover the area where the arm is attached, add a crocheted ruffle:

   a. Using a size G crochet hook, chain 14.

   b. Row 2: Single crochet in each chain.

   c. Row 3: Chain 1 and half double crochet two in each single crochet.

   d. Row 4: Chain 2 and double crochet two in each half double crochet.

   e. Row 5: Chain 1 and half double crochet in each double crochet.

   f. Anchor off, and sew the completed ruffle to the arm at the shoulder.

Because the doll is so colorful, less is more when it comes to clothing her. Besides, you don't want to hide your beautiful collage work underneath layers of clothing. The sample doll is clothed in a simple tutu and a snazzy belt.

1. The tutu is a 20" x 5" (51 x 12.5 cm) piece of tulle. Fold this in half, and hand sew a running stitch along the raw edges. Pull to fit just below her waist, with the opening in the back, then tack in place.

2. The belt is made of two tubes of fabric and a length of yarn that was braided using a Lucet. If you don't have a Lucet, braid some yarn together to the length you want. Measure around her body below her waist to get your measurement.

3. Once you have your tubes and braid made, sew them together at each end, then fit the belt on her body to cover the raw edge of her tutu. Sew in place.

4. At the center, add one joint similar to her leg joints, or add a button or an accent bead.

5. The edging around her bodice is also done on a Lucet. If you don't have a Lucet, make another braid with yarns. Tack this in place. Add an appliqué motif if you wish.

1. Attach mohair to the top of her head, as done in Chapter 3, page 57.

2. Around the mohair, gather a length of the painted lace, and fit it around her head. Then tack it in place.

COLLAGE

Sarah's Symphony

ARTIST: Connie McNabb
 (Pattern: Doll #1)

"I began with a blank canvas—in this case, a piece of unbleached muslin large enough for the body and the costume. Next, I chose fabrics of colors and textures that coordinate. From this cut various sizes and shapes and laid them on my canvas. After the muslin was covered, I pinned the pieces together and zigzagged them together with matching threads. I then scattered bits of threads, trims, and ribbons over the top of this piece and covered that with sheer tulle. I then randomly stitched it all together. After I cut, sewed, and turned the body and firmly filled it with stuffing, I sketched in petal shapes, long enough to create her skirt, on the back of the remaining 'collaged' fabric and completed it with some random beading. I did this before the petals were finished, because I didn't want the thread to show. Finally, I placed sheer organza on top of the petals and used hand-dyed cotton for the lining."

The Lady of Charlotte

ARTIST: Marcia Acker-Missall (Pattern: Doll #1)

"The beginning body gave me a wonderful canvas to work with. After I made the body, I dyed it with several mixed colors, waited for it to dry, and then over-dyed it to give it more texture.

I created the clothing using many types of fabrics and patterns. Collage is such a wonderful technique for creating fun clothing. I used free-motion machine embroidery to make the skirt panels, encasing with thread between two layers of transparent organza various beads, shisha mirrors, and other embellishments. Over this I clustered free-flowing bead embroidery.

The skirt has clusters of fringes to give it movement. The headpiece is a mixture of fabrics and bead embroidery. No-hole glass beads were applied to several areas of the clothing and headpiece to create the effect of brocade cloth."

Maeve

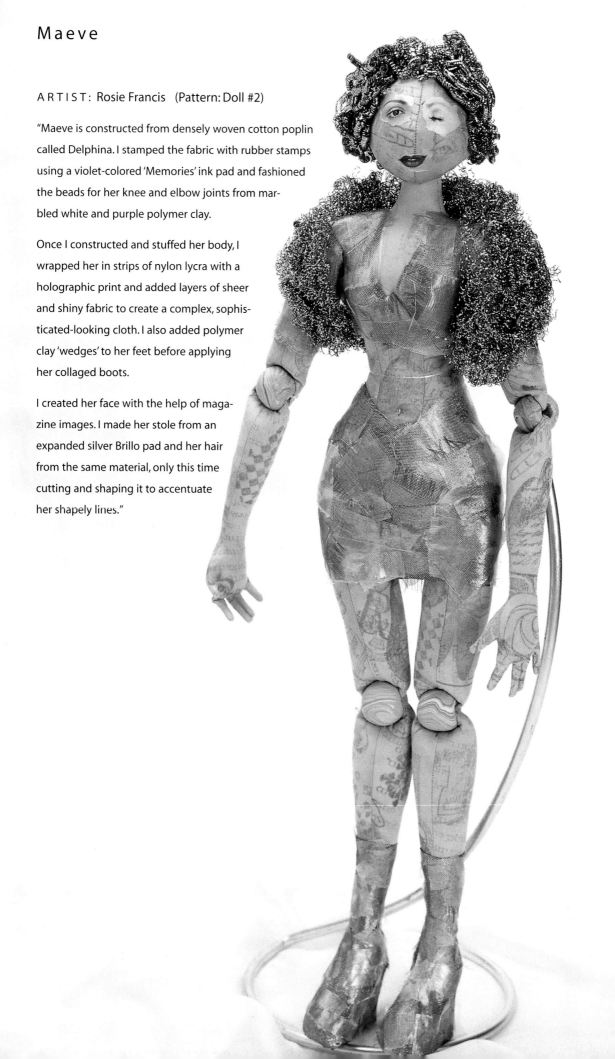

ARTIST: Rosie Francis (Pattern: Doll #2)

"Maeve is constructed from densely woven cotton poplin called Delphina. I stamped the fabric with rubber stamps using a violet-colored 'Memories' ink pad and fashioned the beads for her knee and elbow joints from marbled white and purple polymer clay.

Once I constructed and stuffed her body, I wrapped her in strips of nylon lycra with a holographic print and added layers of sheer and shiny fabric to create a complex, sophisticated-looking cloth. I also added polymer clay 'wedges' to her feet before applying her collaged boots.

I created her face with the help of magazine images. I made her stole from an expanded silver Brillo pad and her hair from the same material, only this time cutting and shaping it to accentuate her shapely lines."

Fionna

ARTIST: Cyndi Mahlstadt   (Pattern: Doll #2)

"When picking out my materials for the collage technique, I started with the velvet leaves, which have shades of peach, pink, salmon, and greens, and worked around them. I used those for my primary colors and added different shades of cream. I also added lacy fabrics, buttons, beads, vintage handkerchiefs, ribbon, ribbon roses, and yarns. Using colors to match my color scheme, I dyed the handkerchiefs, the sheer fabric under the skirt, the ribbon roses, and the big flowers on her head. Then I misted the flowers with water, painted on the dye with a paintbrush, and hung them out in the sun to dry. To give the premade ribbon flowers an antiqued look, I gave them a bath in Jacquard's Dye-NA-Flow paint.

I used no-sew beads in very small sizes. Using a small paintbrush, I applied tacky glue in small amounts and sprinkled on the no-sew beads, then I gently pressed them into place with my fingers.

Costuming this doll involved wrapping and tacking. Her sleeves are made of sheer ribbon wrapped around her upper arms and tacked into place with a needle and thread. I created her skirt from strips of sheer fabric, lace fabric, yarns, ribbon, and handkerchiefs tacked at her waist. I wrapped a fine chenille yarn around her lower arms to finish off her sleeves and at her ankles to finish off her shoes."

Darbi

ARTIST: Jane Coughlan   (Pattern: Doll #3)

"I loved the pattern for Doll #3 because of its interesting exaggerated body shapes, which I knew would work well if I sewed the doll into a fixed pose. I opted for intense colors and lots of busy patterned fabrics, but had no idea what character I was making or who she would be. I just let her lead me along.

To save myself matching the checks and stripes I chose for her legs, I took out the center-front seams. Because I planned to sew the legs in position, I needed the legs to sit around the body rather than on the side (as for button joints), so I added a dart to the outside leg and removed a curve from the inside leg.

After assembling the body and the legs, I colored in the checkerboards on her legs with fabric paint, adding seed beads to the white squares on just one leg. I used a large black and yellow polka-dot print for her skirt and pom-poms, ruffles of tulle, swans down, and decorative yarn for embellishment. Her hair became a veritable prickle bush of cloth spikes, and before I knew it, she'd taken on the airs of a jester."

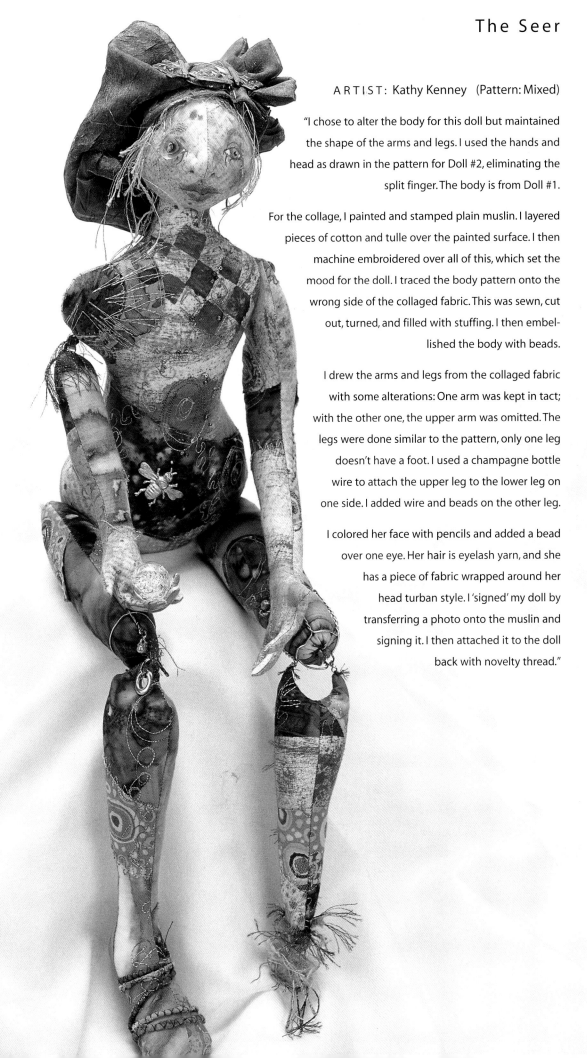

ARTIST: Kathy Kenney (Pattern: Mixed)

"I chose to alter the body for this doll but maintained the shape of the arms and legs. I used the hands and head as drawn in the pattern for Doll #2, eliminating the split finger. The body is from Doll #1.

For the collage, I painted and stamped plain muslin. I layered pieces of cotton and tulle over the painted surface. I then machine embroidered over all of this, which set the mood for the doll. I traced the body pattern onto the wrong side of the collaged fabric. This was sewn, cut out, turned, and filled with stuffing. I then embellished the body with beads.

I drew the arms and legs from the collaged fabric with some alterations: One arm was kept in tact; with the other one, the upper arm was omitted. The legs were done similar to the pattern, only one leg doesn't have a foot. I used a champagne bottle wire to attach the upper leg to the lower leg on one side. I added wire and beads on the other leg.

I colored her face with pencils and added a bead over one eye. Her hair is eyelash yarn, and she has a piece of fabric wrapped around her head turban style. I 'signed' my doll by transferring a photo onto the muslin and signing it. I then attached it to the doll back with novelty thread."

Kara Louise

ARTIST: Bonnie Stewart   (Pattern: Mixed)

"Kara Louise was born from a mix and match of all three doll patterns. Her head, body, and feet are from Doll #1. I loved the wooden bead joints of Doll #2, so her arms and legs came from there. Fingers are a must for me, so I used the hand from Doll #3. I created her hair from the breast pattern from Doll #3.

I cut the body, arms, and legs from the same multicolored fabric. This created her clothing. Her head and hair were from goldenrod-colored fabric. After she was made, I painted Mod-Podge over all to seal the fabric so I could then paint her body. I used Gesso on all parts that were to be her flesh and her shoes. I also added paper clay to her face to give her nose and lips dimension. (This was also covered with Gesso.) I then painted her face and shoes and gave her a bare midriff.

When the paint was dry, I covered the entire doll with many coats of hi-gloss polyurethane, to give her that special china-like look.

For clothing I used seven flower-embroidered handkerchiefs as her underskirt and a crocheted doily as her overskirt. An oval crocheted doily became her jacket. A diamond ring, gold ankle bracelet, and many strands of pearls were all that was needed to complete her."

Julissa

ARTIST: Julie McCullough (Pattern: Doll #3)

"For this doll, I began by pulling all the lime green and fuchsia fabrics off my shelves and laying them out on my worktable. I wanted the body parts to be different, so for the legs I started with flesh-colored fabric as my background. I cut snips of the green fabrics and layered them on the flesh, adding occasional snips of purple and fuchsia fabrics. I wanted her to have bare feet, so I left the bottom edge of the fabric mostly flesh with bits of cream and beige fabric scraps. I added some metallic yarn randomly across the fabric. To this I added a layer of yellow tulle over the fabric and pinned randomly. I used green thread for my stitching.

I started the body and arms with fuchsia fabrics and red-purple tones of scraps. I laid purple tulle on top and stitched with green thread over all. Then I made her skirt from a length of sheer metallic fabric folded in half with a few fabric scrap inserts. Her hat is a stuffed cone shape with a stuffed band around it.

Because I wanted her hair to act as a focal point, I gave her red yarn braids. On her face I gave her eyelids with false eyelashes (the kind you get at the drug store) and my signature—glass eyes."

The Unexpected Angel

ARTIST: Christine Shively   (Pattern: Doll #1)

"Angels come into our lives at unexpected times and in unexpected forms. The opportunity to do a doll for this book came at a perfect time in my life.

Patti and I have a similar appreciation for the seated figure. I wanted to have this figure sit with her arms open and extended. The clothing choices reflect a technique of fabric manipulation that recurs over and over in my own work.

The beading techniques for the added embellishment of this figure are simple. The beaded picot edge shows up everywhere in my dolls. It's the quickest way to bump up a vest, a collar, or a cuff on a doll's clothing.

Another creative joy is to use one simple shape and manipulate it for various uses. Here, a flat wing shape is used in four different places on this figure. I folded the shape in half and created the wings on the back of the doll. I folded it twice to add an interesting shape to the back of her head. I reduced the wing shape and folded it for the skirt. Finding more than one way to use a basic shape is a wonderful way to jump-start your creativity. It pushes your imagination to turn the shape upside down and look at the general shape in a new way."

Genesis

ARTIST: Marguerite Nelson Criswell (Pattern: Doll #1)

"This doll's face is made from four different pictures that complement each other, which I scanned into my computer. After preparing a piece of silk/cotton fabric with Bubble Jet Set 2000, I cut a piece of freezer paper to A4-size paper, ironed the waxed side of the paper to the fabric, and fed it through the printer. I glued the pieces to the stuffed head and dyed the body with Jacquard Textile, Lumiere, and Neopaque dyes.

The arms represent the heavens. The left arm is dyed blues and purples, with white specks to represent stars and space (night). A bracelet with a star charm is on the wrist. The right arm is dyed reds, oranges, and yellows to represent the sun (day), with a sun charm bracelet on that wrist. The legs represent the earth. The left leg is dyed turquoise blues and greens to represent the sea and encircled with copper wire adorned with seashell beads. The right leg is dyed in muted blues and rusts to represent the dry land and is encircled with copper wire adorned with leaf charms.

The hem of the dress is roller-printed with bronze powder in textile medium. I've added Genesis 1:1, 'In the beginning, God created the heavens and the earth,' to the border. The top and sleeves are embellished with Tyvek film painted with various acrylic paints and dyes and bronze powders in different shades of copper.

The angel's hair is made from Thai mulberry and handmade tissue paper roller-printed with acrylic paints, bronze powders, and fabric medium. It's then glued into a lion's manelike hairdo. Her flowing wings are made from three painted layers of Tyvek film—light-weight, medium-weight, and heavy-weight. The finishing touch was finding a paperweight at a local antiques shop that looked like the universe being formed. I placed it in the angel's hands, and she came to life."

The Green Woman

ARTIST: Deb Shattil   (Pattern: Doll #2)

"The Green Man is a pagan symbol of fertility and the cycle of life. His face can be seen in far corners or on ceilings of churches built in the Middle Ages. The costume for this Green Woman was based on sketches of a tree, which inspired the textures, colors, and rhythm of the stitching. Her hair is wrapped to resemble branches. The man always has leaves in his hair, so the woman also wears a little cap of leaves.

Most of the fabrics are enhanced with transfer paints, which are applied to paper, allowed to dry, and then ironed onto fabric. It's important to sandwich your work between sheets of parchment paper to keep paint off your ironing board cover.

The skirt is sheer polyester fabric, roughly cut into a continuous strand 1" (2.5 cm) wide and then loosely crocheted with my fingers. Setting the transfer paint with an iron melted and scorched the fibers. The cycle of life is destructive, so I wanted a degree of disintegration.

The bodice is pink velveteen with brown velvet trim and the sleeves sheer fabric, both with leaves. These are applied with Wonder-under that has been painted with acrylics—a nice way to add a little color here and there.

Perhaps the most courageous act of all was the last. I used a heat gun to burn away some of the chiffon and Wonder-under and further distress the skirt. I then burned the sleeves with a soldering iron. It was exhilarating to spend so many hours crafting a doll just to burn away parts of the costume. This doll was in progress when I attended a weeklong workshop with two British embroidery teachers, Jan Beaney and Jean Littlejohn. This costume design was my final project."

Phoebe

ARTIST: Barbara Willis   (Pattern: Doll #2)

"It was interesting to watch this doll develop step-by-step. I chose to embellish her with knits and crochet as part of my challenge category. Because I don't knit or crochet, I needed to be inventive. As I sat down with Patti's pattern, I realized that I needed to make a few adjustments to the pattern so it would work for my vision of this doll. I reduced it by 20% at a copy center, then I cut away the seam allowances on the torso to slim her up a bit.

As I began to think about her costume and construction, I decided to use a knit fabric to cover the paper clay mask I created for the face. Knit is a perfect fabric to use for this purpose because it molds itself around facial structures. I chose one with a fine-gauge knit, and I used the mesh side of the fabric to represent the skin. It takes color well and works with fine-tip pens. Her legs were made from a small printed cotton fabric. After adding color to the face, I glued the mask in place and button jointed on her arms and legs.

Her costume began to fall into place when I chose silks as the base fabric for the skirt, sleeves, and chest and open-weave gauze for her pantaloons. Using a knitted, man's dress sock, I created a chemise. I cut the sock and added lace to the cut edge. I slipped it up onto her, covering the lower torso and hips over the silk skirt. The knitted sock formed itself to her beautifully, showing off her shape. I added a tassel to embellish the knit chemise and small vintage crochet buttons to embellish the front of the silk bust. Using the leftovers of the sock I created a small knitted cap to cover the back of her head and wrapped silk ties around her face to complete her headdress."

ARTIST: Betts Vidal   (Pattern: Doll #2)

"What would this doll that I was to create be? The answer came when I saw a tiny newspaper ad for a Thai restaurant with a drawing of a graceful, leaping dancer. This would be my inspiration—Thailand! I needed to add my own personal touch, so I began by reducing the given pattern to a size I felt comfortable working with—not too tall, not too small. The pattern featured a broad-cheeked face, a shapely torso, ball-jointed limbs, and squared-off toes. I decided to capitalize on these features.

I began creating the doll with the torso because of the unique piecing. While playing with the pieces, I decided to leave the center panel in a skin-colored fabric. The addition of the lavender bra was a last minute inspiration. This would emphasize her curves and introduce another color. For the face and limbs, I chose a fine ivory silk faille, instead of a traditional flesh color, to emphasize the yellow and lavender silks. I also added my trademark eyelids and eyelashes.

For the beading, I rummaged through my many boxes until I found the perfect vintage lavender bugle beads, yellow and rose crystals, and seed beads.

Part of my creative effort is to name a completed project. Thoughts of the music from *The King and I* and Thailand's original name became 'Song of Siam'—and so my doll was named."

Gynan

ARTIST: Marsha Elam   (Pattern: Doll #3)

"The inspiration for this doll came from the character Whoopi Goldberg played in *Star Trek: The Next Generation*. I loved the hats she wore. A green silk dupioni became the body and a green cotton with gold threads became the legs. Two muted shades of gray/green raw silk form the knickers. I inserted a V-shaped piece into the sides of the knickers to add interest. I frequently repeat shapes when costuming my dolls. It's fun, and you don't need to know a lot about pattern making. I've used this basic shape to make hats, jackets, knickers—just about any piece of clothing. I used the same technique on this doll. The collar, shoes, and hat use the same shape. The knee and elbow joints are a variation of this shape.

I completed most of the beadwork using a brick stitch, because it creates a very tailored edge. What is so cool about beading is that you really don't need to know many stitches. Find one you like, and use it over and over. For the finishing touch on the face, I created wired eyebrows and placed seed beads for added highlights. Lastly, I created a chair for Gynan to sit on."

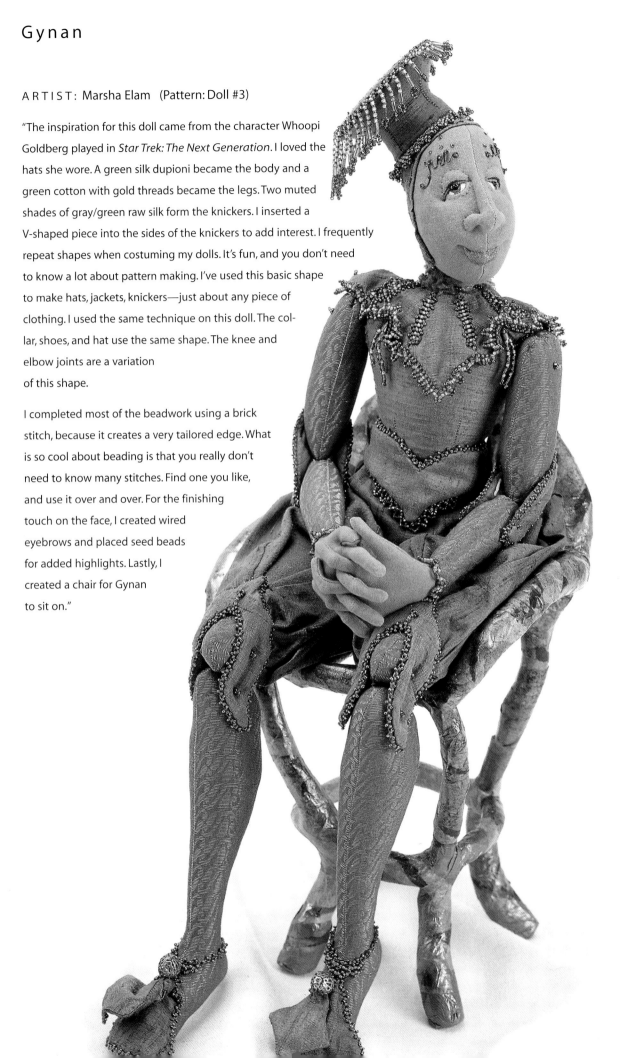

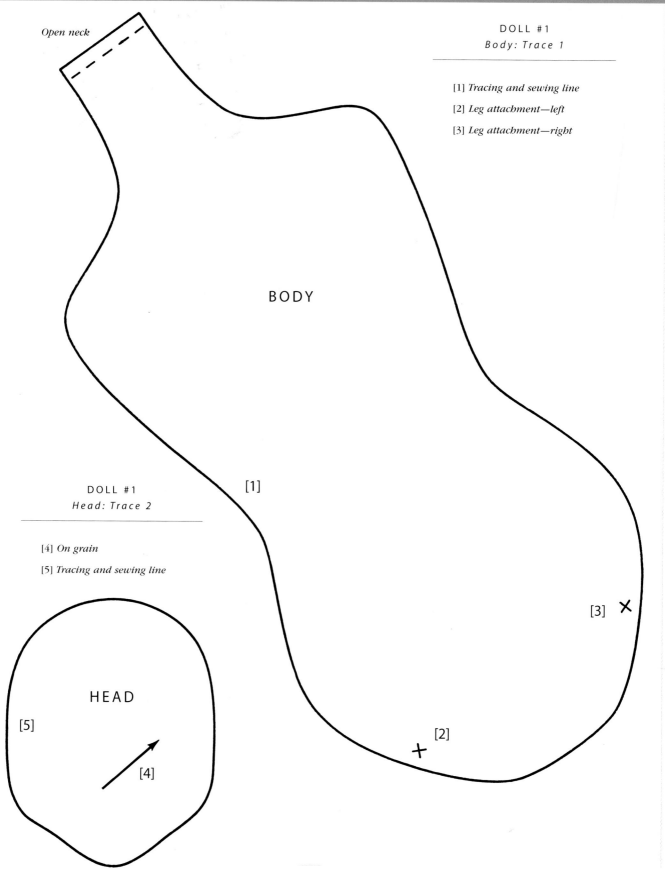

Open neck

DOLL #1
Body: Trace 1

[1] *Tracing and sewing line*

[2] *Leg attachment—left*

[3] *Leg attachment—right*

BODY

[1]

DOLL #1
Head: Trace 2

[4] *On grain*

[5] *Tracing and sewing line*

[3] ✕

HEAD

[5]

[4]

[2] ✕

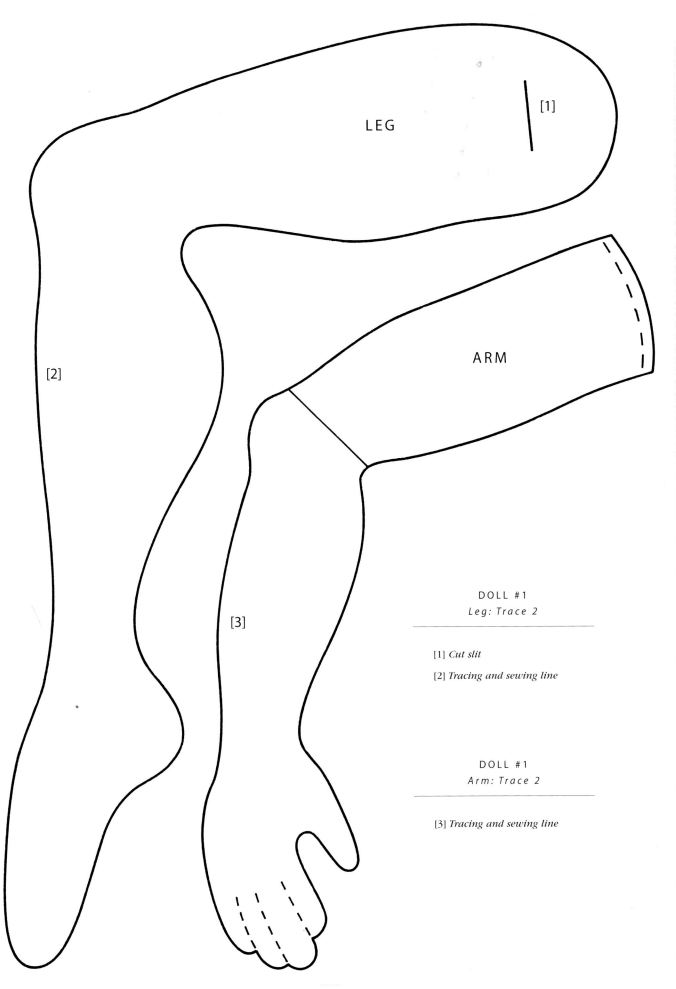

LEG

[1]

[2]

[3]

ARM

P A T T E R N S

DOLL #1
Leg: Trace 2

[1] *Cut slit*

[2] *Tracing and sewing line*

DOLL #1
Arm: Trace 2

[3] *Tracing and sewing line*

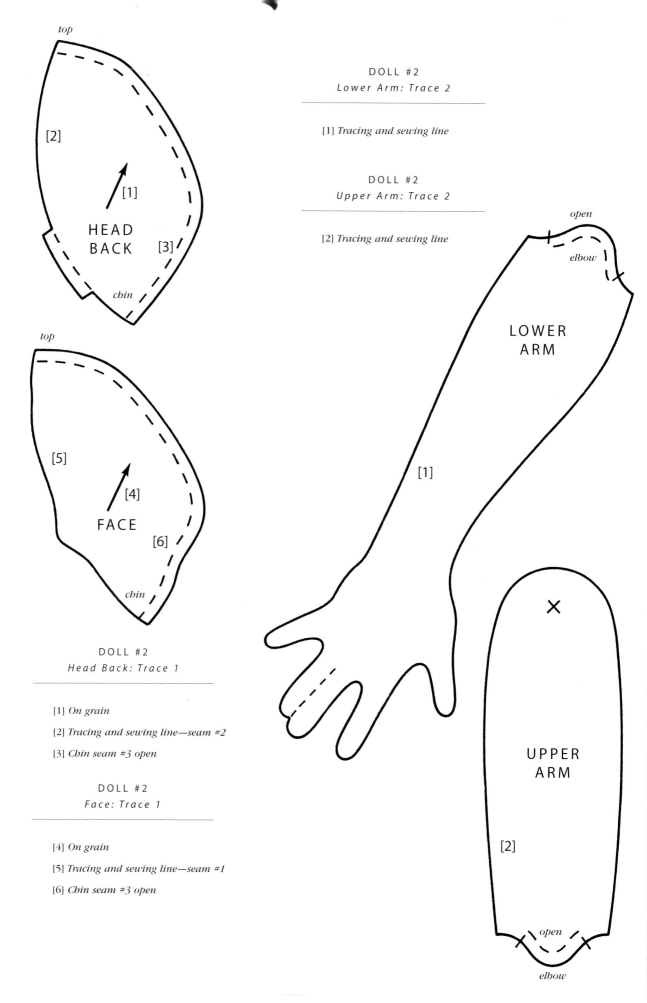

top

[2]

[1]

HEAD
BACK   [3]

chin

top

[5]

[4]

FACE   [6]

chin

DOLL #2
Head Back: Trace 1

[1] *On grain*

[2] *Tracing and sewing line—seam #2*

[3] *Chin seam #3 open*

DOLL #2
Face: Trace 1

[4] *On grain*

[5] *Tracing and sewing line—seam #1*

[6] *Chin seam #3 open*

DOLL #2
Lower Arm: Trace 2

[1] *Tracing and sewing line*

DOLL #2
Upper Arm: Trace 2

[2] *Tracing and sewing line*

open

elbow

LOWER
ARM

[1]

×

UPPER
ARM

[2]

open

elbow

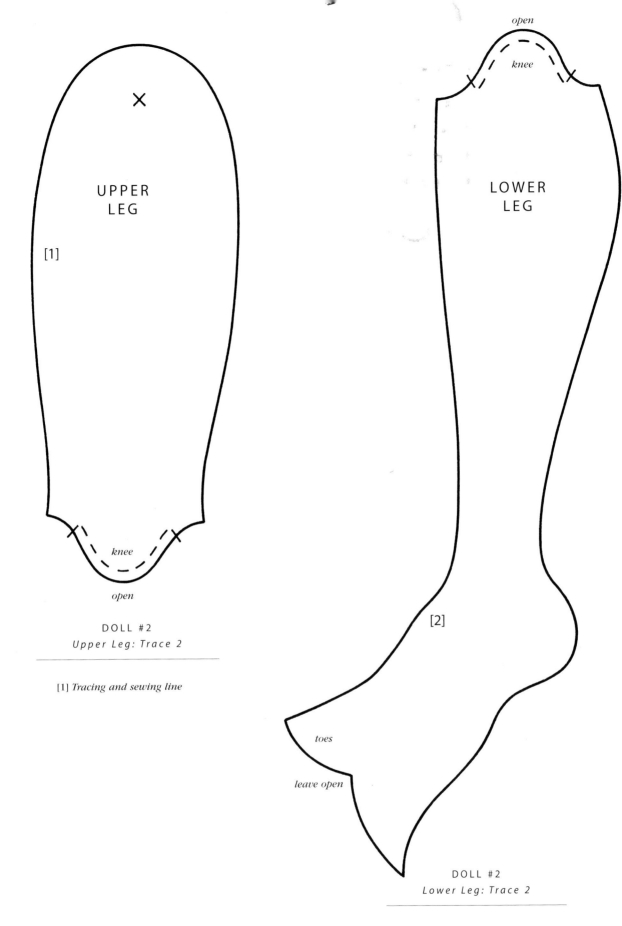

UPPER
LEG

[1]

knee

open

DOLL #2
Upper Leg: Trace 2

[1] *Tracing and sewing line*

LOWER
LEG

open

knee

[2]

toes

leave open

DOLL #2
Lower Leg: Trace 2

[2] *Tracing and sewing line*

DOLL #2
Body Back: Trace 1

[1] *Tracing and sewing line*

[2] *Seam #5*

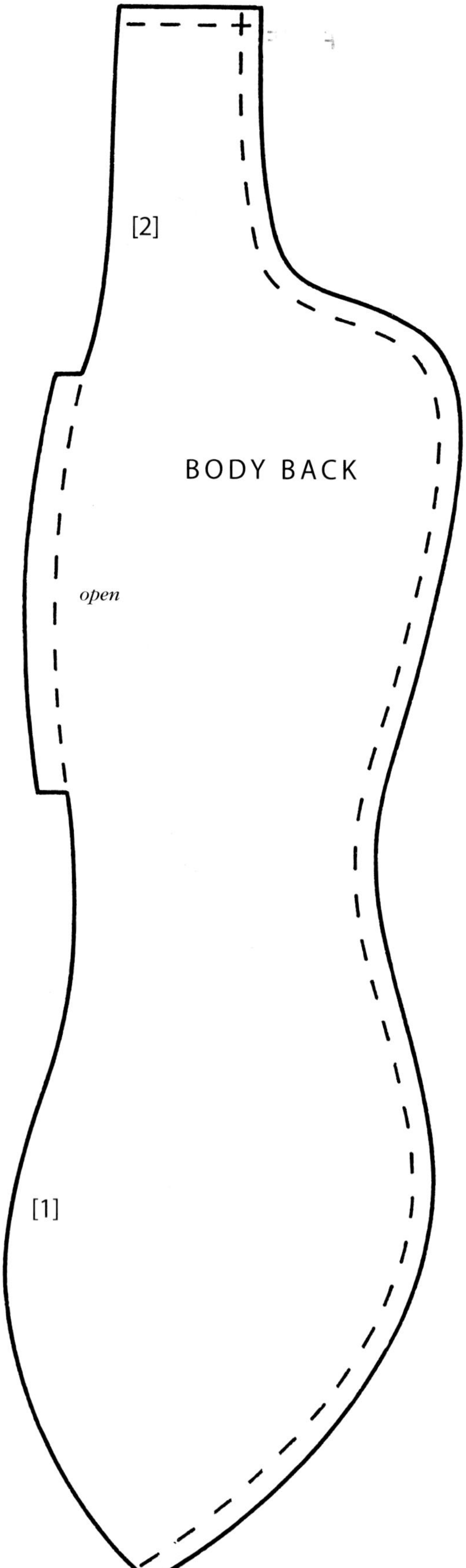

[2]

BODY BACK

open

[1]

DOLL #2
Center Body Front: Trace 1

[3] *Place on fold*

[4] *Seam #4*

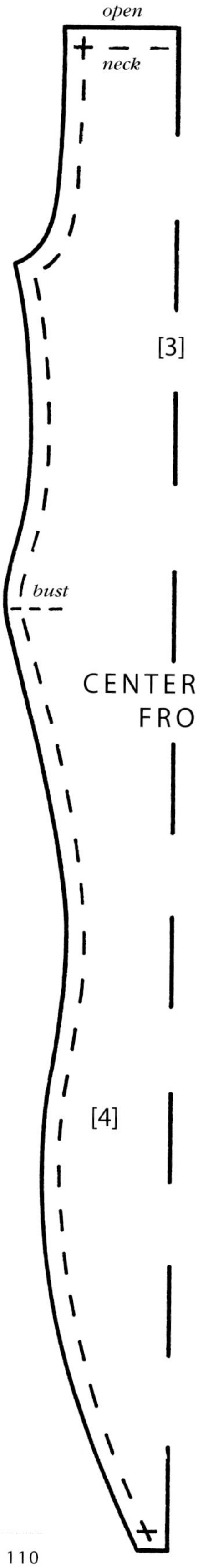

open

neck

[3]

bust

CENTER BODY
FRONT

[4]

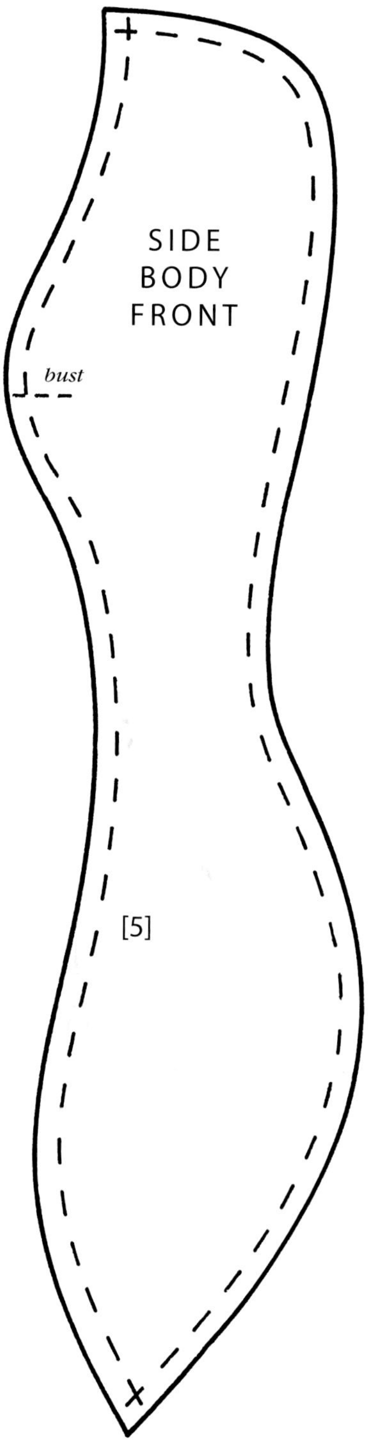

SIDE
BODY
FRONT

bust

[5]

DOLL #2
Side Body Front: Cut 2

[5] *Seam #4*

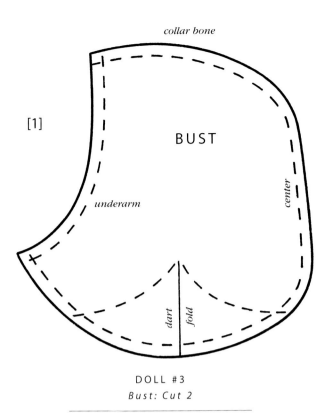

collar bone

[1]

BUST

underarm

center

dart *fold*

DOLL #3
Bust: Cut 2

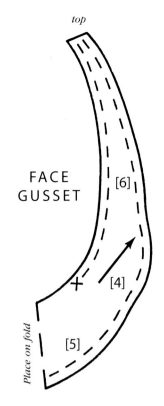

top

FACE
GUSSET

[6]

[4]

[5]

Place on fold

DOLL #3
Face Gusset: Trace 1

[4] *On grain*

[5] *Seam #3*

[6] *Seam #4*

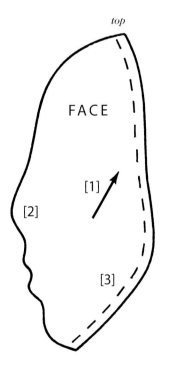

top

FACE

[1]

[2]

[3]

DOLL #3
Face: Trace 1

[1] *On grain*

[2] *Seam #3*

[3] *Tracing and sewing line—seam #1*

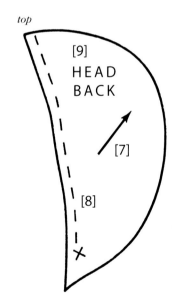

top

[9]

HEAD
BACK

[7]

[8]

DOLL #3
Head Back: Trace 1

[7] *On grain*

[8] *Seam #4*

[9] *Tracing and sewing line—seam #2*

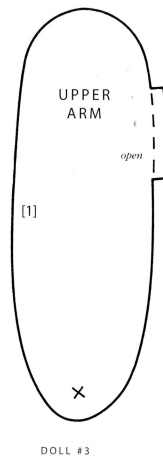

UPPER
ARM

open

[1]

✗

DOLL #3
Upper Arm: Trace 2

[1] *Tracing and sewing line*

ARM & LEG
JOINTS

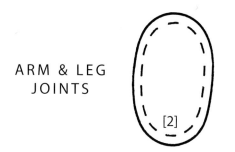

[2]

DOLL #3
Arm and Leg Joints: Trace 2

[2] *Cut 8*

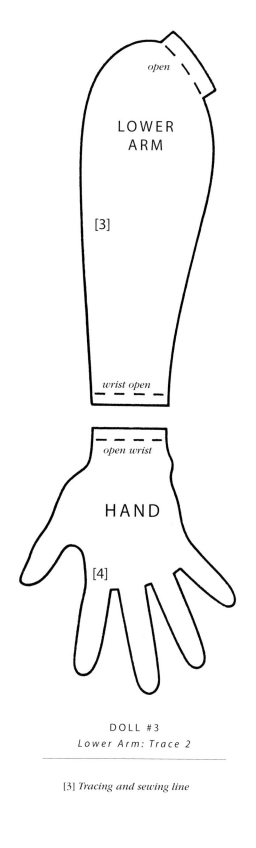

open

LOWER
ARM

[3]

wrist open

open wrist

HAND

[4]

DOLL #3
Lower Arm: Trace 2

[3] *Tracing and sewing line*

DOLL #3
Hand: Trace 2

[4] *Tracing and sewing line*

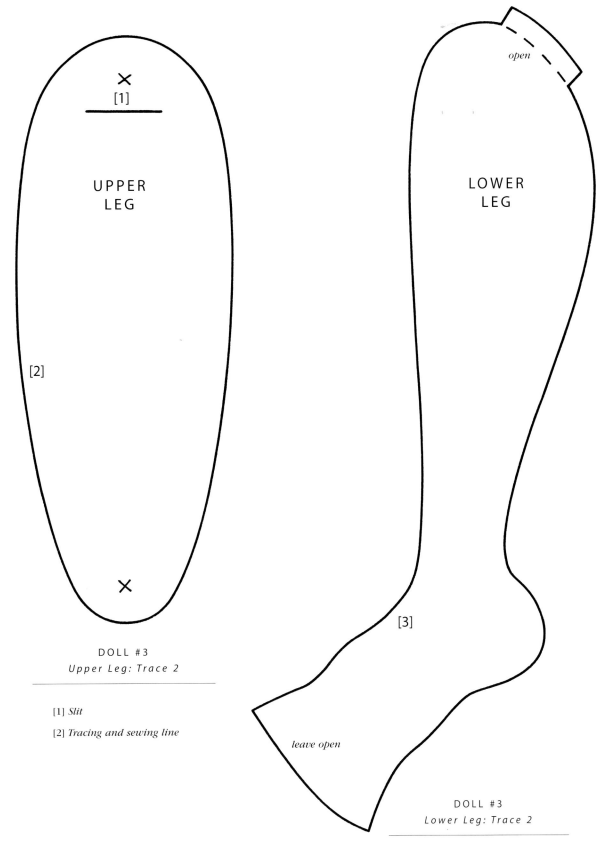

UPPER
LEG

✗

[1]

[2]

✗

DOLL #3
Upper Leg: Trace 2

[1] *Slit*

[2] *Tracing and sewing line*

LOWER
LEG

open

[3]

leave open

DOLL #3
Lower Leg: Trace 2

[3] *Tracing and sewing line*

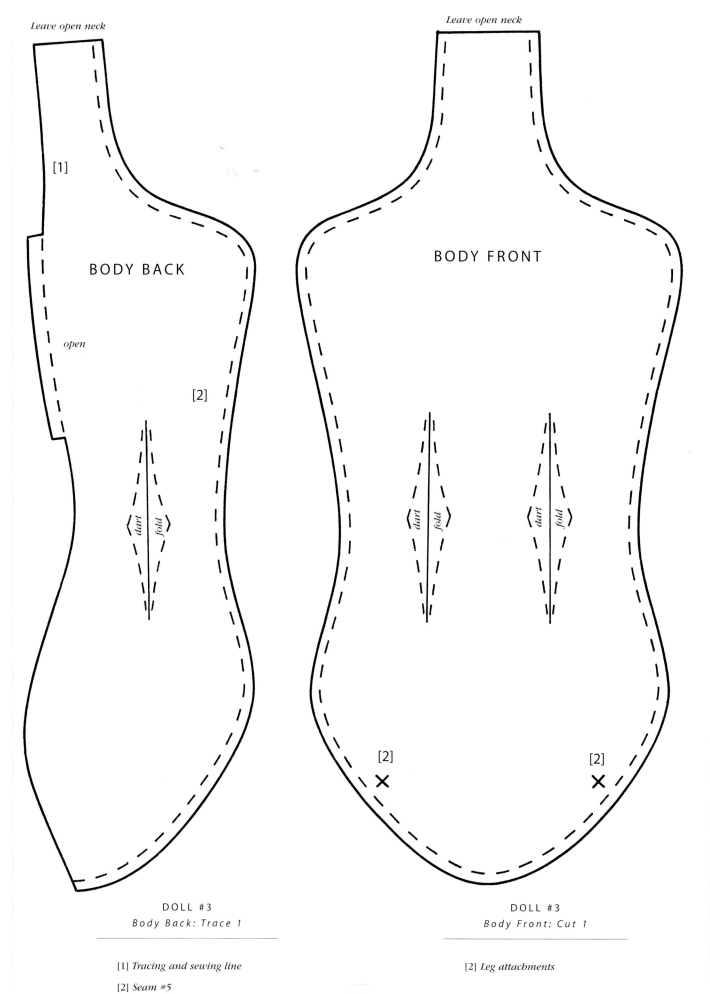

Leave open neck

[1]

BODY BACK

open

[2]

dart *fold*

DOLL #3
Body Back: Trace 1

[1] *Tracing and sewing line*

[2] *Seam #5*

Leave open neck

BODY FRONT

dart *fold*

dart *fold*

[2] [2]

✕ ✕

DOLL #3
Body Front: Cut 1

[2] *Leg attachments*

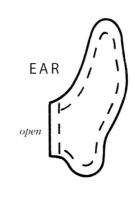

EAR

open

OPTIONAL PIECES FOR ALL DOLLS
Ear: Trace 2

WING
TEMPLATE

OPTIONAL PIECES FOR ALL DOLLS
Wing Template: Trace 2

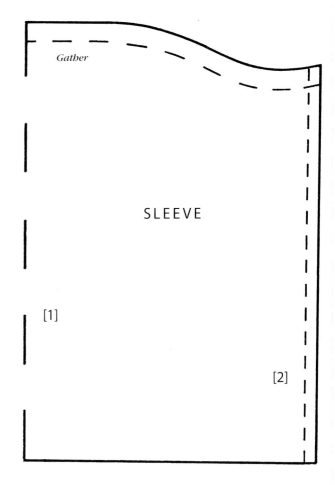

Gather

SLEEVE

[1]

[2]

OPTIONAL PIECES FOR ALL DOLLS
Sleeve: Cut 2 on fold

[1] *Place on fold*

[2] *Seam #1*

115

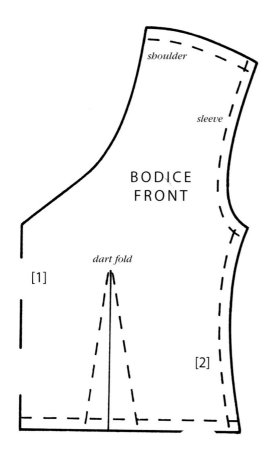

shoulder

sleeve

BODICE
FRONT

dart fold

[1]

[2]

OPTIONAL PIECES FOR ALL DOLLS
Bodice Front: Cut 1 on fold

[1] *Place on fold*

[2] *Side seam*

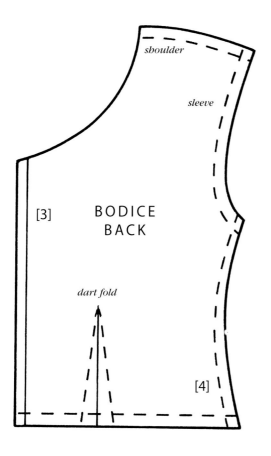

shoulder

sleeve

[3]

BODICE
BACK

dart fold

[4]

OPTIONAL PIECES FOR ALL DOLLS
Bodice Back: Cut 2

[3] *Back opening*

[4] *Side seam*

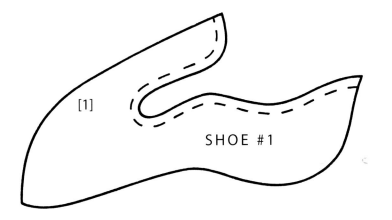

[1]

SHOE #1

OPTIONAL PIECES FOR ALL DOLLS
Shoe #1: Trace 2

[1] *Tracing and sewing line*

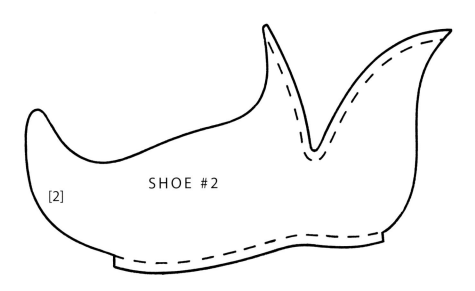

[2]

SHOE #2

OPTIONAL PIECES FOR ALL DOLLS
Shoe #2: Trace 2

[2] *Tracing and sewing line*

SHOE #2
SOLE

OPTIONAL PIECES FOR ALL DOLLS
Shoe Sole: Cut 2

Resources

United States

Cloth Doll Connection

For online doll-making needs
web site: www.clothdollconnection.com
Designers, online classes, calendar of events

Doll Heaven

Lisa Risler
2590 FM 356
Trinity, TX 75862
936-594-6703
web site: www.clothdollpatterns.com
email: lisadawn@wt.net
Patterns, supplies, Yadeno Mohair, online classes

"Impress Me" Stamps

Sherrill and Joel Kahn
17116 Escalon Dr.
Encino, CA 91463
818-788-6730
web site: www.impressmenow.com
email: impressmenow.com
Wholesale and retail rubber stamps
Catalog: $5.00 (refundable on the first order)

Meinke Toy

724 Sylvanwood Ave., Suite 1
Troy, MI 4885
248-813-9806
web site: www.meinketoy.com
Tyvek, books, threads, stabilizers

PMC Designs

9019 Stargaze Ave.
San Diego, CA 92129
858-484-5118
web site: www.pmcdesigns.com
email: jculea@san.rr.com
Patterns, tools, newsletters, classes, one-of-a-kind dolls

Rupert Gibbon & Spider

P.O. Box 425
Healdsburg, CA 95448
1-800-442-0455
web site: www.jacquardproducts.com
email: jacquard@sonic.net
Jacquard products—Dye-NA-Flow paints, Lumiere paints, textile paints, Pearl-EX pigments, silk fabric, photo transfer fabrics

Things Japanese

9805 N.E. 116th St., Suite 7160
Kirkland, WA 98034
425-821-2287
web site: www.wilkthings.com
email: thingsjapanese@seanet.com
Colorhue Silk Dyes, Silk Ribbon

Tsukineko, Inc.

17640 N.E. 65th St.
Redmond, WA 98052
425-883-7733
web site: www.tsukineko.com
email: sales@tsukineko.com
All Purpose Inks, Brilliance stamp pads

Australia

Anne's Glory Box

60-62 Beaumont St.
Hamilton
NSW 2303 Australia
049 61 6016
web site: www.textiletraders.com.au/agb
email: annesglorybox@bigpond.com.au
Fabrics, dyes, beads, books, stabilizers, mohair

The Thread Studio

6 Smith St.
Perth
Western Australia 6000
61 8 9227 1561
web site: www.thethreadstudio.com/index.htm
Threads, metallics, Tyvek, stabilizers, books

Yadeno Fibre Craft

J & L Digweek
The Summit
Queensland, Australia
07 4683 2485
email: Yadeno@halenet.com.au
Beautifully clean mohair in natural and
many colors

United Kingdom

Art Van Go

1 Stevenage Rd.
Knebworth,
Herts SG3 6AN
01438 814946
web site: www.artvango.co.uk
email: art@artvango.co.uk
Jacquard products, Tyvek in all weights

Calico Pie

(Mail order only)
015396 2195

Craft Depot

(Mail order only)
0145827 47 27

Hobby Craft

(Stores nationwide)
Head Office
Bournemouth
01202 596 100

John Lewis

(Stores nationwide)
Flagship Store
Oxford Street
London W1A 1EX
0207 629 7711
web site: www.johnlewis.co.uk

Rainbow Silks

6 Wheelers Yard
High Street
Great Missenden
Bucks HP16 OAL
01494 86211
fax: 01494 86265
web site: www.rainbowsilks.co.uk
Jacquard's Dye-NA-Flow paints

The Yorkshire Art Store

10 Market Place
Pickering, North Yorkshire YO 187AA
0800 195 7440
fax: 01751 475 626
web site: www.yorkshiresartstore.co.uk
Jacquard's Dye-NA-Flow paints

Further Reading

Angel Crafts
by Holly Harrison
Rockport Publishers
ISBN 1-56496-852-9

Creating with Paint
by Sherrill Kahn
Martingale & Company
ISBN 1-56477-320-5

The Stamp Artist's Project Book
by Sharilyn Miller
Rockport Publishers
ISBN 1-56496-762-X

Stitch Magic
by Jan Beaney and Jean
Littlejohn
Quilter's Resource
ISBN 1-889682-04-7

Surfaces for Stitch
by Gwen Hedley
Batsford Ltd.
ISBN 0-7134-866-X

Textile Dyeing
by Kate Broughton
Rockport Publishers
ISBN 1-56496-839-1

Contributors

Marcia Acker-Missal

18228 Clear Brook Circle
Boca Raton, FL 33498-1945
561-852-3858
potdfrog@bellsouth.net
web site: www.pottedfrog.com
Pattern designer, workshops

Known for her wonderful beadwork, Marcia Acker-Missall has developed a line of doll patterns incorporating this technique. Marcia holds a BFA from Cooper Union School of Art, Architecture & Engineering and has done graduate work at Hunter and City Colleges. She has worked for *McCall's* magazine as an artist/designer and has taught fine art in New York City. Today, Marcia teaches beading and cloth doll making and has had work featured in the magazine *Belle Armoire*.

elinor peace bailey

1779 East Ave.
Hayward, CA 94541
510-582-2702
epb@prado.com
web site: www.epbdolls.com

elinor peace bailey has been designing patterns for about 27 years and publishing and teaching for 20. Her dolls are an outgrowth of her fancy for the human figure. She began as a painter and found a passion for fabric, which begged a third dimension. This, of course, required that she learn to sew. A combination of twists and turns introduced her to the quilt world, where she's been mentored and inspired by the best. elinor designs fabric and her work has been published in magazines and books worldwide.

Lynne Butcher

P. O. Box 537
Coolum Beach, Queensland 4573
Australia
61-7-5446-3904
lynnebutcher@dingoblue.net.au
Pattern designer, workshops

Lynne Butcher has been designing and teaching cloth doll making for many years. She began her career as a school-teacher, specializing in art, and now spends much of her year on the road selling her patterns, teaching workshops, and designing.

Lynne is a member of the National Original Doll Artists of Australia. She has won many awards, among them the Diamond Gold Seal by NODAA. In 2000, she was inaugurated into the Doll Hall of Fame at Doll-O-Rama.

Barbara Chapman

353 Glenmont Dr.
Solana Beach, CA 92075
858-755-4451
Workshops

Barbara Chapman has been a fiber arts teacher in the San Diego area for more than 30 years. She and her husband, Wayne, a potter and glass bead artist, open their home twice a year to sell their work as well as the creations of other artists exhibiting wearable art. Barbara avoids sewing machines whenever possible, preferring hand sewing. In fact, many of her early dolls were collaged together with glued fabrics and much embellishment.

She now enjoys paper clay as a medium for creating faces, because it accepts paint so well. Surface decoration is her first love—fantasy expressed in color and texture. Her journey continues in search of that little spark that invites her into a magical world. It's there where her imagination becomes reality.

Jane Coughlan

P.O. Box 34
Waitakere, Auckland 1250
New Zealand
64-9-810-9385
dollmajc@icarus.ihug.co.nz
Pattern designer, workshops

Jane Coughlan is an internationally recognized textile artist who has been at the forefront of modern cloth doll making in New Zealand since 1993. She designs and makes cloth dolls and quilts full-time and publishes designs for her mail-order business, Red Hot Rag Dolls. She also teaches cloth doll making regularly in the United States, Australia, and all over New Zealand. She has won a number of awards over the years for her quilts, dolls, and wearable art, and has been part of five group exhibitions.

Marguerite (Margie) Nelson Criswell

52 Weldon Rd.
Marston, Oxford OX8 0HP
UK
01865-240122
criswell@btinternet.com

Marguerite (Margie) Nelson Criswell began making dolls in 1988 and painting in 1994 as creative outlets for stay-at-home motherhood. As she discovered that art was a means to express her identity and calling, she developed a desire to use it to communicate her Christian faith. She works with fabric sculptures, watercolors, pastels, and colored pencils. Her fabric sculptures incorporate fabric sculpting, painting, wire work, beading, stamping, collage, printing, and embroidery. Born and raised in Ellenton, Florida, she now lives in Oxford with her husband and two children. Her artwork can be found in private collections in England, Canada, and the United States. The Isis Gallery in Oxford represents her artwork. She holds a Bachelor of Science in Business Education and a Master of Arts in Religion.

Janet Beth Cruz

21 N.W. 101st St.
Miami Shores, FL 33150
305-756-6250
jblacruz@aol.com
One-of-a-kind dolls

From an early age, Janet Beth Cruz had a passion for creating something from nothing. In high school, she won first place at a local county fair for her first oil painting. Like her mother and others from her family, portraits were of great interest to her. One of her high school classes was in sewing, and she really loved that—especially the fashion design element. Today she continues to learn and experiment in both fine and fiber arts. Janet made a doll for each bridesmaid who was in her wedding.

Marsha Elam

5410 So. Land Park Dr.
Sacramento, CA 95822
916-446-2076
Workshops
One-of-a-kind dolls

Sacramento, California, has been Marsha Elam's home for 30 years. She works part-time as a paralegal, and in her off time she creates magical cloth dolls. Although she has been making dolls for several years, she wasn't exposed to the creative process of making original dolls from scratch until she joined a doll club. Marsha says that although she became a serious doll maker after that, she generally doesn't make serious dolls. She specializes in needle sculpting and costuming. She's in demand as a teacher throughout the western states, and she'll soon expand her horizon to the rest of the world.

Barbara Carleton Evans

124 Poli St.
Ventura, CA 93001
805-648-3860
BarbeDolls@aol.com
Workshops

Barbara Carleton Evans's early childhood was spent with a family of dolls. They were her constant companions for tea parties, walks to the beach, and adventures into rhododendron-filled forests surrounding her home. In later years, she continued making dolls—from clothespins, flowers, and other found materials. Soon she abandoned commercial patterns and began designing her own. She moved from fabric to felt, hand-made felt, found objects, natural materials, beads, and anything else that looked fun.

Her work has found its way into craft and doll magazines, books, craft and art shows, and stores. She now designs dolls using various media, although paper is quickly replacing fabric as her material of choice. It can best be said that her dolls develop "organically," emerging from the very nature of the materials themselves.

Wendy Fenwick

5 Mt. Pleasant Ave.
Mona Vale 2103
NSW Australia
61-02-9999-4616
fenwicks@attglobal.net
Workshops

Wendy Fenwick lives in Sydney, Australia. She has two beautiful daughters and a wonderful husband of 32 years. Sewing, fiber arts, and creative pursuits are a very important part of her life. She's addicted to color, texture, and textiles. Along with her passion for sewing, she has tried many arts and craft forms, always returning to her love of wearable art, patchwork and quilting, cloth dolls, garment construction, machine embroidery, and felt making. She also loves knitting and designing one-off creations using various yarns. Beading, incorporating machine embroidery, is her latest foray, and although it's the most time-consuming, it has given her yet another dimension of artistic expression.

Rosie Francis

23 Wilson Dr.
Ottershaw, Surrey
KT 160 NT England
01932 873590
rosiered@usa.net
Workshops

Rosie Francis has been interested in textiles since her early years. Her passion grew as she spent more time exploring the skills that her mother and grandmother imparted to her as a young girl. After leaving Australia and traveling to the Middle East, she further explored art and culture, allowing these things to influence her work and art. Today Rosie is part of the Tri This Design Group with Janet Twinn, Dianne Robinson, and Hilary Gooding.

Kathy Gaines

9850 Garfield Ave., #81-A
Huntington Beach, CA 92646
714-962-2113
gainesx2@thegrid.net

Kathy Gaines's first remembrance of sewing was on a doll for charity as a young girl in Sunday school. Things really haven't changed much for her: She still sews on her little baby sewing machines, only now it's with her collection of baby Featherweights.

She has always loved the needle arts and believes that she can apply everything she has learned in the past—china painting, ceramics, porcelain dolls, needlepoint, machine knitting, crochet, stained glass, silk ribbon embroidery, quilting, beading, silver work and jewelry making—to doll making. She especially loves to make dolls that are movable and depict the innocence of childhood. She's a member of various cloth doll clubs and has never lost her enthusiasm for making dolls for children.

Margaret (Marge) Gorman

1841 Rolling Hiss Rd.
Sacramento, CA 95864-1671
916-487-9878
mgo1414087@aol.com
Pattern designer, workshops

Margaret (Marge) Gorman was born in and now resides in Sacramento, California. She's a wife and mother of four who owns and operates Mrs. Sew & Sew, a home-based business dedicated to designing original cloth dolls. Marge is President of Tayo's Doll Works morning Doll Club.

She teaches doll making and has won numerous awards for her whimsical dolls. She has been published in several *Cloth Doll Magazine* articles. One of her dolls was featured on the July 2000 cover of *Soft Dolls & Animals* magazine and another was accepted in the 1999 national Hoffman Exhibit.

Annie Hesse

124 Broadmoor Dr.
Daphne, AL 36526
334-626-3888
dolls@zebra.net
Pattern designer, workshops

Annie Hesse has been making and selling mixed media and fabric figures since the mid-eighties. Before that she was a basket maker, which eventually led her to doll making. Annie says it was the knarly vines and branches she used. Each day she'd look at them and wonder. Finally she grabbed a bunch of them, tied them together, lashed another one across for an arm, added a huge lichen-like fungus that resembled a head, and called it her first doll. After that, she just let it flow, making figure after figure and adding other mediums, like fabric, to these sculptures.

Annie has given up her secure, tenured job as a high school teacher to make dolls for a living. She now teaches her techniques worldwide, exhibits in galleries, does a few art shows a year, has pieces at the White House, and does commissioned work for movies and television shows.

Kathy Kenney

1082 Hollister Dr.
Kent, OH 44240
330-678-7923
kkenney@neo.rr.com
One-of-a-kind dolls

Kathy Kenney is a retired graphic artist who now creates contemporary cloth dolls. Her dolls are a collage of all the things that interest her—hand-painted fabrics, bright contemporary cotton prints, machine stitching, and unusual embellishments.

Dorice Larkin

19463 Oriente Dr.
Yorba Linda, CA 92886
714-777-5550
DoriceL@aol.com
Pattern designer, workshops

Dorice Larkin, in a humble understatement of her gifts, says she has been "playing with art" all of her life. In college Dorice studied textile design and theater arts. Her devotion to starting a family put her art on hold for many years, and now she and her husband, Bill, have five adorable girls. It was while playing with her daughters that she was drawn back to her art, this time through doll making.

What draws Dorice the most to doll making are the people involved in this art form—including their love of sharing their ideas as well as their "stash." Dorice finds most of her inspiration from her dreams, her books, and her daughters. She has a commercial line of patterns that are both whimsical and realistic.

Eileen Lyons

405 N.W. 70th St.
Boca Raton, FL 33487
561-997-2186
eplyons@bellsouth.net
Workshops

Eileen Lyons has been making dolls for years. She started out making cute little country dolls and then moved on to "art dolls." She's a member of a wonderful doll club in sunny south Florida called the Sanddollr's. This group brings in many doll artists throughout the year, which has broadened Eileen's outlook on dolls. Eileen works full-time and uses doll making as a way to relieve the stress. Eileen says that doll making will be her retirement joy whenever she slows down—and that will be something to see!

Julie McCullough

439 W. Chestnut St.
Lancaster, PA 17603
717-399-3972
Julie@magicthreads.com
web site: www.magicthreads.com
Pattern designer, workshops

Julie McCullough has been a fiber artist for more than 25 years. She started out as a weaver and spinner, doing soft sculpture dragon ladies. Now she's a doll maker and pattern designer.

Julie is known in the quilting and doll-making world for her unique hair treatments, bold colors, and whimsical subject matters. She likes clean designs with geometric elements.

In 1989 Julie started designing and marketing a line of doll patterns under her business name Magic Threads. She now teaches from her home studio in Lancaster, Pennsylvania. Her work has been featured in many magazines, on TV shows, and in several books on dolls. She enjoys making one-of-a-kind dolls and dolls and cloth sculpture props for stage productions.

Di McDonald

11 ColJohn St.
Landborough 4550
Queensland, Australia
FAX 07 549 31028
di@dyzee.com
Pattern designer, workshops

Di McDonald was born in New Zealand and has been living in Australia for the past 10 years. Her background is in fashion design and clothing manufacturing.

Di works in the fabric arts full-time, teaching, designing, and drafting patterns (mainly in the human form). She has a website and publishes a quarterly newsletter to help promote cloth doll making and artists from all over the world. She teaches online classes through her website and also hosts other teachers.

Connie McNabb

18455 S.W. 84th St.
Miami, FL 33157
305-255-7900
conniescraft@aol.com
One-of-a-kind dolls

Connie McNabb began making dolls 15 years ago. Her first were from patterns by Elinor Peace Bailey and Patti Medaris Culea. She now creates original and award-winning dolls, many of which have been featured in *Soft Dolls & Animals.*

Cyndi Mahlstadt

619 Collins Ter.
Escondido, CA 92026
760-489-1283
Cyndi@mygrammasgarden.com
web site: www.mygrammasgarden.com
Workshops, one-of-a-kind dolls

Art has always been Cyndi Mahlstadt's passion—sketching, sewing, and making things. In 1995, Cyndi started making cloth dolls, teaching herself the basics. After that she started exploring different techniques, in an effort to develop her own style. In January 2001, she discovered wire armature figures, and a whole new world opened. Overnight, she was hooked!

Cyndi enjoys making fantasy figures. Much of her inspiration comes from her garden and from nature. She often includes a touch of whimsy and humor in her work. The technique she enjoys most is "cloth over wire" for bodies and needle sculpting for faces. Going back 20 years, Cyndi says that "making dolls as an art form never crossed my mind." Today, it's her joy and passion!

Ann Maullin

P.O. Box 344
Newcastle, NSW 2300
Australia
61 2 65 791028
annmaullin@cardiovasc.com
Pattern designer, workshops

Ann Maullin lives in the Hunter Valley vineyard region in the state of New South Wales in Australia. She's married to a wonderful man, Greg, and has two children and two grandchildren. A figurative fiber artist who loves creating with this medium, she has been designing her own dolls since she started making them 6 years ago.

Claudia Medaris

1064 Curtis St.
Albany, CA 94706
medaris@hotmail.com
Paper/stamp artist

Claudia Medaris graduated from the University of California at Berkeley, where she studied ceramics with Peter Voulkos. She produced pottery in the San Francisco Bay area for many years and now continues to produce graphic art, mainly rubber stamp creations. Her work has been published in *Somerset Studio, Rubberstampmadness,* and the *San Francisco Chronicle.*

Claudia is an active member of the Capolan Exchange, a renowned Mail Art group, and her personal essays on the nature of the artistic mind are a regular feature of *The Studio* and the *BrainWaves OEZine.* Residing in Albany, California, Claudia is married and the mother of two daughters.

Michelle Meinhold

1750 E. Barndon Lane
Fresno, CA 93720
559-434-8434
meinhold@csufresno.edu
Bead artist, workshops

Michelle Meinhold discovered her love of color while studying fine arts at the University of California Santa Cruz. The color choices in textiles and beads have helped fuel her creative fires. At first she used beads to embellish the dolls. One day the obsession took over, and beads became her medium of choice. To satisfy her need to make dolls, her Floral Tassel Doll series came into bloom. She has been a cloth doll artist since 1985; she began teaching cloth dolls and beading in 1998.

Kandy Scott

403 S. 6th
Canadian, TX 79014
806-323-9178
kandy@bow.net
One-of-a-kind dolls, workshops

Kandy Scott's dolls are eclectic and incorporate many different techniques—a style that she attributes to her short attention span disorder. Taking workshops in free-motion surface design, fabric dyeing, and beading has also helped her create fun dolls. She says she wants the viewer to look closer and discover the surprises in each piece. Using old jewelry, sewing on soda cans, manipulating painted Tyvek, and attending to details makes her dolls fun to look at again and again.

Kandy now teaches workshops on her techniques, makes dolls for auctions to benefit local interests, and does some consignment work for family and friends. At the time of this writing, Kandy is preparing for her first one-woman show at a gallery near her home in Texas.

Deb Shattil

9200 Skyline Blvd.
Oakland, CA 94611
510-482-0340
rshattil@juno.com
One-of-a-kind dolls

Deb Shattil earned a bachelor's degree in sculpture at the University of South Dakota. After graduation, a master weaver hired her to work on large, commissioned tapestries and to weave a series of small tapestries made from hand-spun buffalo wool. She continued to weave her own designs for another 10 years.

In 1992, she discovered contemporary cloth dolls and was inspired to make her own. It fused her love for textiles, sculpture, and the human figure. Photographs of her work have been included in five books, and she sells dolls in galleries and stores across the country. In 1999, she was one of 80 doll artists in the United States invited to make and donate an ornament for the White House Christmas tree. She looks forward to doing more teaching and is on a committee that organizes a national cloth doll conference. She has lived in California for 20 years with her cat and wonderfully creative husband.

Christine Shively

8717 Hilltop Rd.
Ozawkie, KS 66070
785-876-2804
shively@ruralnet2.com

Born and raised in Denver, Colorado, Christine Shively, the second of six children, loved art even at an early age. In college she studied many different art forms and eventually settled on the human figure in cloth. She started showing her work in 1984 at the Kansas City Renaissance Festival. It was events like this that led her to pursue a career in doll making. Today, Christine shares her love of doll making by teaching at various doll events throughout the United States, Australia, and New Zealand. She also participates in fine art fairs throughout the United States. Christine says that the sense of adventure and independence that this venue gives her has helped expand her horizons artistically and organizationally.

Bonnie Stewart

2775 Snow Partridge Dr.
Reno, NV 89523
775-747-7574
blsdolls2@aol.com
One-of-a-kind dolls, workshops

Bonnie Stewart is a self-taught doll maker who says she owes all that she has learned and achieved to the wonderful and talented members of the Imitation of Life Construction Company, a cloth doll society. These members encouraged and inspired Bonnie to grow, improve, and try new things.

Bonnie is mostly known for her painted and glazed dolls that have a distinct chinalike look. Her dolls have been published in magazines, including *Soft Dolls & Animals*. She has won many awards through the Hoffman Challenge, doll exhibits, and county fairs. Her dolls have traveled in the Figure in Cloth doll exhibit.

Ute Vasina

4000 N. 15th St.
Lincoln, NE 68521
402-435-3969
ute@neb.rr.com
web site: www.enchantingdelights.com
Pattern designer, workshops

Born and raised in Germany until age 12, Ute Vasina never had much interest in sewing—until her daughter was born and she got the urge to sew her a dress. But it wasn't long before she went from sewing dresses for little girls to sewing dolls.

She attended a doll show with her mother, where she saw cloth dolls up close. Soon after, she joined a local doll club known as the Mad Dollmakers; this group helped her grow as a doll maker and designer. Because of her fascination with trolls, she started researching these characters and creating them herself. Each of Ute's trolls is uniquely different and full of life. Ute's creations have been featured in *Soft Dolls & Animals* magazine and the Figure in Cloth doll exhibit.

Betts Vidal

26163 Underwood Ave.
Hayward, CA 94544
510-782-9390
bettsvidal1@earthlink.net
Pattern designer, workshops

When Betts Vidal was at the tender age of 18 months, her parents placed a small chalkboard 18" (45.5 cm) from the floor to encourage her to draw. To this day, she can sketch a thought easier than she can articulate one. Studying art, painting, drawing, interior design, pottery, basketry, lapidary, and quilting—as well as having a love of natural elements, richly textured fabrics and surfaces, luscious colors, Americana, buttons, and found objects—all led her to the world of doll making. Dolls are a lifelong way of incorporating all she has experienced into a most rewarding form of creativity. The dolls have taken her to many new places, to other countries, and to treasured friendships. And best of all, her husband, children, grandchildren, siblings, and parents all share in her delight of dolls.

Barbara Willis

415 Palo Alto Ave.
Mt. View, CA 94041
650-962-0639
bewdolls2@aol.com
web site: www.barbarawillisdesigns.com
Pattern designer, workshops

Dolls have been a part of Barbara Willis's life for as long as she can remember. She settled on cloth dolls after a few seasons with porcelain and never looked back. She comes from a creative family that sewed, decorated, painted, and loved fabric. She has fond memories of haunting the fabric stores with her grandmother and mother. She has been creating these treasures for many years and enjoys the pleasures of teaching in the United States as well as internationally.

About the Author

Patti Medaris Culea grew up on a farm in Illinois, where artistic family members nurtured her creative talents. Among them was an uncle who was an animator for Walt Disney, who later helped her get a job at Disneyland. After studying art in college and working as a portrait painter, Patti spent many years as a flight attendant traveling throughout the world, including time with Flying Tigers, transporting military troops to Vietnam.

After making dolls for her two daughters, her love of fiber arts took hold. She attended classes in doll making and has since become an internationally known instructor. She also designs one-of-a-kind dolls and her own line of doll patterns available through her website, www.pmcdesigns.com. She and her husband, John, have been married for 29 years. They reside in San Diego, California.

Acknowledgments

My thanks go to my husband, John, for his continued support, encouragement, and editing help. Also, to my daughters, Janet and Heidi. Heidi gave me ideas and JB made a doll for the book. Thank you to JB's husband, Luis, for encouraging her to do it. Thanks go to my parents, Bob and Fran Medaris, who continue to be proud of what I'm doing. Heartfelt thanks also to the artists who contributed to this book. They jumped in with enthusiasm and created wonderful dolls beyond what I could ever have imagined.

This book would never have happened without the help of my editor, Mary Ann Hall. Thank you, Mary Ann, for your extraordinary, gentle patience. Thanks also to Winnie Prentiss, publisher at Rockport, whom I worked with during Mary Ann's maternity leave. During the development of this book, both became proud parents of their own, real life dolls, baby boys.

Finally, best wishes to those of you who are reading this book, especially if you are about to make one of the projects. I'm so excited for you and the fun you're going to have. We are members of a family, people who are linked with creativity and a love of cloth dolls. I wish I could see each of your finished products. I know they'll be fantastic.